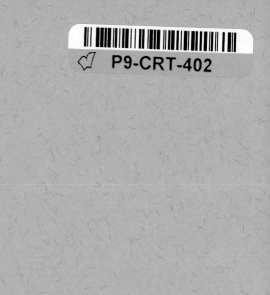

TUCK & TUCKER

TUCK

&TUCKER

The Origin of the
Graduate Business School

Wayne G. Broehl, Jr.

Benjamin Ames Kimball Professor of the
Science of Administration Emeritus

University Press of New England

HANOVER AND LONDON

Published by University Press of New England, Hanover, NH 03755

© 1999 by Wayne G. Broehl, Jr.

Printed in the United States of America

5 4 3 2 1

CIP data appear at the end of the book

Acknowledgments

With appreciation to the Rauner Special Collections Library of Dartmouth College for use of its holdings of Edward Tuck and William Jewett Tucker letters, photographs, and memorabilia, as well as general Dartmouth College materials, including the Franklin Brooks papers. Photographs of James J. Hill courtesy of James J. Hill Group, Saint Paul, Minnesota. For specific citations, please contact the author at Dartmouth College.

Thanks to Robert Fisher (T '48) for his generous gift that made this publication possible.

Cover photograph: Edward Tuck. Courtesy Dartmouth College Library.

Contents

Illustrations

Foreword

A simple idea—giving broadly educated students the education needed for a career in business leadership—formed the origin of the MBA degree. The values Dartmouth president William Jewett Tucker and Mr. Edward Tuck articulated over one hundred years ago led to the creation of the Amos Tuck School of Business Administration in 1900 and remain at the heart of our efforts today. The needed education, then as now, must be an immersion in business thinking, where students learn from leading scholars and from each other; it must be broad-based; and it must have a global perspective, with inputs from diverse cultures.

In its first hundred years, Tuck has graduated 7,033 talented women and men who have taken up leadership positions in virtually every form of organization in all parts of the world. The Tuck School's noble experiment spawned today's massive graduate business education industry, with thousands of MBA programs, with millions of MBA degree holders, and with growing worldwide demand for its talented graduates.

Today, top business schools such as Tuck have global reach. In addition to the traditional residential experiences, students now benefit from action learning in global business settings and from contact with faculty who are experts in the world's best business practices. Also, a huge array of degree and nondegree offerings are delivered by means of media that could not have been imagined in 1900. Technology is eliminating many limitations of time and space in the transmissions of ideas and data. One thing is certain—these global and technological revolutions will both mold the future of business schools and create intriguing challenges.

Tuck will combine the best of our traditions with an aggressive program of innovation, intelligent deployment of technology, and worldwide partnering with leading corporate and academic institutions. We will honor the Tuck and Tucker heritage by treating every student and alumnus as an exceptional individual and by maintaining the highest standards. We will meet the challenges of the future not by growing to the huge scale of our competitors but by leveraging the techniques and technologies of the new era.

Tuck's first class started with only four young, bright Dartmouth students. Tuck's one hundredth class is composed of 191 students from around the world. They are diverse and enormously talented individuals, who have an average of five years experience. The program fosters teamwork, contact with business leaders, and interaction with the enormously loyal Tuck alumni—all of which goes beyond ordinary education. The MBA program of today transforms the student in terms of aspirations, career paths, and even lifelong friends.

Wayne Broehl's book chronicles how, at the dawn of the twentieth century, Mr. Tuck and President Tucker conceived of and launched a powerful educational movement. The Tuck School will lead that movement into the twenty-first century.

PAUL DANOS
Dean, Amos Tuck School of Business Administration

TUCK & TUCKER

Mr. and Mrs. Edward Tuck. Courtesy Dartmouth College Library.

"I Wish to Do Something for Old Dartmouth"

So wrote Edward Tuck to William Jewett Tucker on October 21, 1898: "I see by the papers that the Dartmouth Trustees have long urged you to take a leave of absence in which to get needed rest and recuperation." No one, said Tuck, had taken a greater interest or satisfaction in the recent success of the college than he. "My thoughts often recur with pleasure to the days of our college intimacy, especially that winter term of 1860–61 when we roomed together. I hope that in your busy life you have not entirely forgotten them." Expressing a wish to "do something for Dartmouth," Tuck enclosed a check for $1,000, which he hoped that the Tuckers would use as part payment of the expenses of their proposed vacation. Tuck urged a trip abroad, perhaps a Mediterranean trip, and closed with an enigmatic sentence: "I would like very much to see you, for many reasons."

Dr. Tucker had gone on from graduation to become an ordained minister in the Congregational Church and was by this year of 1898 president of Dartmouth College. Tuck, after his graduation, first became an American diplomat stationed in France, then a highly successful financier in a firm operating in both New York and Paris. In 1889, Tuck had retired permanently to a set of residences in Paris and elsewhere in France.

In April 1899, President Tucker and his wife, Charlotte Cheever Tucker, visited Edward and Julia Tuck in their home in Paris; it was the two men's first contact after a hiatus of over thirty-five years. The reacquaintance of the two old friends soon led to a gift from Tuck to Dartmouth College of quite substantial size. The trustees of the college designated several uses for this grant; by far the most important led to the path-breaking decision on January 21, 1900, to establish the Amos Tuck School of Administration and Finance as a two-year graduate school, the first of its kind in the entire country. Thus, the Tuck School became the precursor of one of the most important of modern-day advanced educational efforts, the ubiquitous American graduate business school, conferring today's widely known MBA degree.

Fascinating events had taken place in the lives of these two men prior to this seminal renewal of their friendship in 1898. Many of these experiences had much relevancy for Tuck's benefaction to the college and the resulting new graduate school. A brief description of these will enrich the reader's understanding of those exciting days, both before the important gift and after. The focus here is on the earlier events in the lives of these two men and on the inception and early days of the Tuck School through its first quarter-century, up to the death of President Tucker in 1926. Edward Tuck lived a dozen more years, to 1938; some of his later experiences also will be included.

Heresy and a Simmering Controversy

Graduating from Dartmouth College in 1861, one year before Tuck, William Jewett Tucker stepped out into a country beginning its terrible Civil War. An early bout with typhoid fever rendered him unable to qualify as a soldier in the hostilities ("a lifelong regret," he later wrote). First, Tucker accepted a teaching post in Columbus, Ohio. However, the ministry increasingly drew him, and in 1864 he entered Andover Seminary to train to become a pastor in the Congregational Church. Almost immediately, he was given a leave of absence by the seminary to enable him to serve with the United States Christian Commission as an orderly among the wounded of the western army at Chattanooga under General William Tecumseh Sherman. Later, when Sherman left for his historic march through Georgia, Tucker was discharged from the commission and returned to the seminary to complete his studies for the divinity degree. Ordained in 1867, he was called to the Franklin Street (Congregational) Church in Manchester, New Hampshire. In 1875 a much more prominent post suddenly came available, and Tucker went to the

William Jewett Tucker's graduation picture, Dartmouth class of 1861. Courtesy Dartmouth College Library.

Madison Square (Presbyterian) Church in New York City. This assignment was a plum, for the church was what today likely might be called a cathedral church. Its congregation included Cyrus Field of Atlantic cable fame and Samuel J. Tilden, governor of the state of New York.

Nevertheless, parish ministry was not to be Tucker's niche in the world of religion. In 1880, Andover Seminary proffered Tucker a position on its faculty, at a salary less than half that of the Madison Avenue post—and he took it. By this time, Tucker also had become involved in Dartmouth affairs in a major way; a Dartmouth alumnus wrote to a friend about him: "You remember he left a ten-thousand dollar pulpit to accept a professor's chair at Andover on $3,000. He is clear and modern and remarkably honest for a minister, too."

In 1875, Dartmouth gave Tucker an honorary degree of doctor of divinity, and in 1878 he was elected a trustee of the college, coinciding with the new presidency of Dr. Samuel Bartlett. In one of the best biographies on Tucker, *Dr. Tucker's Dartmouth*, authors Richard F. Leavens and Arthur H. Lord commented on Bartlett as "sincere, accepting personal hardships in his devotion to the College . . . [but] temperamentally dogmatic and antagonizing. Equally disturbing . . . was the fact that his scholarly ability and attainments belonged to an intellectual system no longer prevailing." Bartlett was antagonistic to anything that had to do with the theories of Darwin. As the two biographers put it, "he was brilliant as an exponent of doctrines fast becoming archaic."

Bartlett's personal qualities and backward thinking had caused increasing trouble with both the alumni and the faculty (although, perhaps surprisingly, not so much with the students). As contention flared, the trustees tried to keep the peace (with Tucker working actively on this cause). All through Tucker's time at Andover he was dealing with an acrimonious, increasingly hard-line set of positions among constituencies at Dartmouth College. Unfortunately, it never lessened during Bartlett's presidency, despite the good offices of Tucker, particularly.

There was worse to come, and it involved Tucker personally. "When I returned to Andover in 1880 . . . I found no sign of the impending controversy," Tucker recounted later. But it surfaced within months. Back in the first decade of the 1800s, while accepting a grant for new buildings and additional faculty posts, the seminary had volunteered to add to its constraints an outside "Board of Visitors." This three-person group had separate, seemingly overriding influence over the seminary's own trustees. The board was narrowly conservative and soon took exception to the liberal leanings of five of the seminary's senior staff, one being Tucker. As positions hardened and personal animosities grew, the Board of Visitors finally moved against one of the five, and the other four were pulled into this first controversy. In a convoluted set of moves, the Board of Visitors eventually brought charges of heresy against all five.

These doctrinal charges mirrored the religious tensions of the times. This was a period of "great preachers" moving around the country representing various, often diametrically opposed, doctrinal postures, and religious hairsplitting was widespread among a great many people. An accusation of heresy is almost inherently complicated; the Andover altercation was just this, involving both pointed religious charges and ongoing personal animosities expressed by the Board of Visitors toward the five professors. The board succeeded in muddling the situation further by claiming they found that the Reverend Egbert Smythe, the leader, "seems to conceive of truth poetically rather than speculatively," and this "rhetorical quality would interfere with [Smythe's] position as a teacher." The trustees of the seminary and most of its faculty saw the issue clearly as a threat to theological freedom and rose up collectively in affront.

The accused five had already made plans for the publication of a new journal, the *Andover Review*, "hoping there to be able to treat all of the issues carefully and in restraint." However, the secular press jumped on all the details of the squabble, and the "theological wags" (Tucker's term) soon made it a national news story. Finally, after many more months of tortuous religious and legal stratagems the courts became involved, questioning the legality of the attempt by the Board of Visitors to unilaterally make so many decisions for the seminary. The five Andover professors resoundingly won their case, and the whole brouhaha was abruptly put to rest by the court decision. The five had had their "progressive orthodoxy" affirmed, winning in the process "reasonable assurance of theological freedom," a view held by Tucker and most of the rest of the faculty. Professor Leon B. Richardson, author of a two-volume history of Dartmouth College, summed up one of the key issues in this confrontation: "[E]special animosity was aroused by the refusal of the professors to subscribe to the doctrine that infants and those of heathen races, who have never enjoyed the opportunity of listening to Christian teaching, are necessarily condemned to eternal perdition. This lenient attitude toward such unregenerate individuals was sneeringly called the 'doctrine of a second probation.'. . . . The missionary organizations asserted . . . that 'universal perdition of the heathen is the real basis of missions' and that it was hardly to be expected that large expenditures for the conversion of such peoples could be secured if later they were to be given another opportunity for salvation." The outcome of such a position was "ludicrous," Richardson pronounced, and that was essentially the conclusion of most observers.

Tucker seemed not to have suffered personally from the disagreeable court case. As the two authors of *Dr. Tucker's Dartmouth* put it, "he was recognized as a heretic—or a liberal, or a progressive—depending on the speaker's predilections." To quote Tucker's own phrase, his theological position was expressed in those two words: *Progressive Orthodoxy*, the title of a book published in 1886 with nine articles by the five members, Tucker writing three. Tucker was progressive not only in theology but in "social economics," a course he had established at Andover to refocus the church's social concerns from its concentration primarily on charity to that of economic justice. It was one of the first courses of this type for seminarians in the country. One of his noteworthy students in this effort was Robert A. Woods, who had become motivated by Tucker to turn his attention from the ministry to social work as a profession and was instrumental later, with Tucker, in founding a settlement house, first called Andover House but in 1895 renamed South End House to identify it with the depressed section of Boston where it was located.

In February 1892, President Bartlett resigned his post as the head of Dartmouth. Tucker attended that meeting and was disconcerted when the other trustees forthwith elected him president of the college, without so much as a by-your-leave. His remonstrations seemed to be of no avail: Tucker had come through both the Andover controversy and Dartmouth's problems with its presidency with all the constituencies at both institutions solidly, indeed unequivocally, dedicated to his leadership. But Tucker felt he owed Andover his return there to help bring about normalcy and finally was able to persuade the Dartmouth board that they could not just summarily take him away from Andover. He returned to the seminary, and the Dartmouth trustees reluctantly began the search for a new president.

The quest went on unremittingly throughout the remainder of 1892 but failed to produce any results. The situation at Dartmouth appeared to become progressively more compromised, and Tucker worried: "I could not altogether put by the disturbing feeling that, as the outcome of my decision was beginning to show, I had chosen the easier rather than the more strenuous course." So Tucker relented, and in February 1893 agreed to accept the presidency of Dartmouth College.

A "New Dartmouth"

"There was nothing in the previous training or interests of Dr. Tucker," said Leon Richardson in his monumental history of the college, "which could give reason for the belief that he would be especially skilled in the conduct of affairs. Immediately upon his assumption of the presidency, however, he showed powers of vision, adroitness in management, breadth of view, and sheer daring which made him the unquestioned leader of a Board of Trustees, many of the members of which were men whose life work was that business and who had had been highly successful in such matters."

Tucker quickly became aware of the electric force latent in the college—what he came often to call "the corporate consciousness of the College." He saw in the Dartmouth polity a readiness that could allow him to grasp the moment. The enthusiasm and dedication that was lying quiescent within the strong bonds of tradition at the college was just ready to be released (he hoped) for a dramatic upsurge toward a "New Dartmouth." The facilities at the institution, he felt, were meager, the place "altogether in educational crisis." In his inaugural address and in other speeches and writing at that early point of his leadership, he exuded boldness of purpose as well as enthusiasm and self-confidence. Indeed, his policy was so bold that Richardson was moved to comment, "Not all could perceive its wisdom, and men were not wanting who pronounced it over-venturesome." One student in a history department examination paper compared Tucker to founder Eleazar Wheelock by positing that both were "gamblers by instinct." Tucker, when told of this, replied, "I was as much pleased as amused with the insight of the student."

In his frequent writings about the status of the country's private colleges, Tucker was no Pollyanna about their shortcomings. Many of these institutions he saw as narrowly loyal and provincial, sometimes even anti-intellectual. This applied in part to the Dartmouth of the period just before Tucker. Often it appeared that its biggest alumni boosters sat on their hands when it came time to follow their professed loyalties with hard cash for their Dartmouth. Tucker wanted to plan not just for the next ten years but for the next fifty. He laid down challenges for reconstructing the physical plant, modernizing its infrastructure, and expanding it, calling particularly for new dormitories, laboratories, and classrooms. Altogether, Tucker galvanized the college community—faculty, students, and alumni—to join in effecting the New Dartmouth that he had envisioned for them. In this he couched everything in terms of the basic inherent idealism of colleges. In Tucker's wonderful autobiographical book, *My Generation*, he described "corporate consciousness" this way: "When the college man of today really enters into this consciousness, and is really touched by the sense of vocation with which he has been called, he is 'stung by the splendor' of the same thought that inflamed the hearts of the men of the Middle Ages." One can see how a great many people could join with this sincere, remarkable man!

By the first half dozen years of Tucker's tenure as president, a whirlwind of activity on both the physical and the intellectual sides of the college had taken place. There was a steady, satisfying trend line upward in enrollment; in September 1893 the matriculating class was more than twice that of the year before, and by 1899 the student body had almost doubled from that of 1892: 627 and 315, respectively. Tucker was fundamentally dedicated to strengthening the curriculum and finding men of the caliber to teach this new work. By 1899 the curriculum had expanded to twice its size of six years previously, and the faculty had more than doubled, from 19 to 44. Tucker also surprised everyone with his instinct for and adroitness at finance. He especially wanted to develop the college's "earning power." The alumni were tapped, and the state of New Hampshire itself made contributions each year in the 1890s, amounting to some $45,000 in total. Bequests by alumni began to pick up, too. Tucker particularly focused physical expansion on dormitories. (An interesting collateral to this was the establishment by the college and the town of Hanover of a water system, allowing indoor toilets in college dormitories for the first time.) In Tucker's fifth year, 1897, a separate, self-standing dormitory, Richardson Hall, was erected; some of the suites had private baths, a real luxury for the lucky residents.

All of this had happened prior to the event with which we opened—the first contact between William Jewett Tucker and Edward Tuck since they had been roommates over the winter of 1860–61, thirty-seven years earlier. Now Tuck acted. But before we see the form this action took, a brief look at Edward Tuck's life to this date (1899) is in order.

Edward Tuck: The Early Years

Edward Tuck was a product of New Hampshire, born in Exeter. His father, Amos Tuck, was a lawyer and thrice represented the state in the U.S. Congress. Amos was an Independent Democrat when there was not yet a Republican party in the country (the Whigs and the Free Soilers were the key predecessors). With the prevailing conservative politicians of New Hampshire, sparks often flew.

Edward, born in 1842, graduated from Phillips Exeter Academy in 1858. Following in the footsteps of his father, who was a Dartmouth College graduate of the class of 1830, Edward matriculated at the college in 1859 with sophomore standing in that critical year just before the beginning of the Civil War. Throughout his Dartmouth career he roomed alone, with one important exception. Life was not easy for the Dartmouth students of that day, with no central plumbing and, worse, no central heating. Tuck wrote Tucker many years later: "Your

Edward Tuck's graduation picture, Dartmouth class of
1862. Courtesy Dartmouth College Library.

description of the past winter in Hanover carries me back to the winter of 1861–2 when I was the sole occupant in the North Building
during the winter term. Well do I remember wading through the
deep snow to and from the Western door (also the Eastern), the icy
cold building and the wood fire in the Franklin stove that I bought of
Dan Rollins [Daniel G., class of 1860], whose room I had inherited."

The single time that Edward Tuck shared accommodation at

Dartmouth was, of course, the winter term of 1860–61, with Tucker. When Tuck originally broached the idea to his father, the latter was cautious. Tuck explained to his father:

> One of the Seniors, Tucker, who has a very cozy room out of the buildings and whose chum is, and is to be, absent teaching, has invited me very cordially to stop here this winter and room with him. . . . He is a model young man, standing 3rd in his class, and holds a position, which requires a recommendation from the Profs, of the best sort, i.e., he is the only tutor in Mrs. Sherman's select school for young ladies. [John K. Lord, in his history of the town of Hanover, mentions that "Miss L. J. Sherman had a small school in the little building on the north side of the lane leading to the cemetery, near where South Massachusetts Hall now stands." Tuck called it the "Sherman Nunnery" in a letter to Tucker in 1908.] . . . He is a very fine fellow, intellectually and morally . . . follows up his professions and reads his bible every night."

Amos Tuck was impressed, and he consented. Edward took to the relationship with considerable gusto. But in the spring he chose to remain alone in a room on the third story, southwest corner, of the deserted Thornton Hall, and this displeased Amos.

Edward graduated second in his class in the spring of 1862, earning a Phi Beta Kappa key and giving the class oration at the ceremonies. But he and all his classmates graduated into the teeth of the war. His father was single-minded that Edward take a position of responsibility that would maximize his educational qualifications; the first choice of Amos was entrance to West Point for an officer's commission. The senior Tuck had many excellent connections in Washington, and in particular was a good friend of Abraham Lincoln (indeed, Lincoln had visited the Tuck residence on occasion before his election as president). Amos penned several letters, including one to Lincoln: "He is nearly 19 years old . . . stands near the head of his class . . . is of good stature, uses no tobacco, drink, no intoxicating liquor, and gives his father no anxiety." But the fact that Edward was not yet twenty was an impediment. A West Point commission and other similar assignments that Tuck the elder felt were worthy of his son's

Amos Tuck, Dartmouth class of 1835, in 1859. Courtesy
Dartmouth College Library.

interest required that age. Despite excellent backing by Lincoln and
others, the authorities were not willing to bend such a rule.

By 1863 the draft was in place and casting a shadow over thousands of young men, Edward Tuck included. At this point, Amos
Tuck made a decision that Edward should buy his way out of the
draft by providing a substitute. This approach was widespread at the
time; more than 26,000 men had already availed themselves of such

an alternative that year. Edward paid $400 for his exemption, significantly over the usual fee of $300 (the extra amount "perhaps went to a broker," surmised Franklin Brooks, one of Edward Tuck's biographers; the demand for substitutes had risen, driving the price up). This mandated choice of Amos seemed to bother Edward in later years, as Brooks noted: "Neither this account [an Edward Tuck autobiographical effort, written in the 1930s] nor others that he authorized long after the event refer to West Point, the draft, or a substitute. His decision to leave the war behind him was an embarrassment that he chose to avoid."

Edward then tentatively decided to read for the law—a natural choice, following the profession of his father. However, he had to seek medical attention for poor eyesight, which required him to give up the goal of working toward being a lawyer. After a stint in the grocery business in Louisville, Kentucky, and a short assignment in St. Louis as a broker in cotton, he decided to leave for Europe. He traveled on the Continent with friends, then passed an examination in 1864 for consular clerk for the American government, the assignment to be in Paris, a city he already had come to love. The consul at that time was John Bigelow, formerly the editor of the New York *Evening Post* and a skilled diplomat who became a mentor for Edward. In December 1864, the minister, W. L. Dayton, suddenly died. Bigelow became acting minister (later minister) and appointed Edward as acting consul and then consul.

A unique new job then surfaced. Tuck had met John Munroe in Paris; he was head of the firm bearing his name, a prestigious, medium-sized financial institution with offices in New York and Paris, and dominant in the financial flows between the two cities. In 1866, Munroe asked Tuck to join the firm, and Tuck accepted with alacrity. He seemed to have a natural instinct for the intricacies of finance, a flair for business, and a capacity for sustained hard work. Quickly, he became a trusted associate and, by 1871, a partner in the firm, an obvious coup for a young man of twenty-nine. A year later, in 1872, he married Julia Stell, a wealthy young American heiress, the adopted daughter of William S. and Anne Eliza Stell. Stell was a prosperous and successful American merchant banker, with offices

Julia Stell Tuck. Courtesy Dartmouth College Library.

in Manchester and London. When Julia once again was orphaned, in 1867 at the age of seventeen, "with an inheritance of around £100,000" (according to Franklin Brooks), she began living in Paris as ward of George E. Richards, the Paris head of the Munroe firm, and it was there that Edward met her.

The job Edward Tuck held was lucrative, and its earnings were combined with managing Julia's money; he finally chose to retire altogether from active business at the end of the year 1881, at age thirty-nine. His Munroe work had been in New York, where he and

Julia had established a home at 2 West 61st Street, but they visited Paris a number of times, eventually taking a small apartment on the Champs-Elysées. In 1889 they decided to move to France permanently and soon had a spacious apartment at another location on the Champs-Elysées, No. 82 (known all through the American expatriate community simply as "82"). It became not only the center of social activity for Americans but increasingly a favorite for the French

The Tucks' country home, Château Vert-Mont, commune of Rueil-Malmaison, eight miles from Paris. Courtesy Dartmouth College Library.

intelligentsia, such as diplomats, businesspeople, and high government officials. As Beckles Willson, a prolific Canadian writer of history with an apartment in Paris near the Tucks, put it, Tuck had become "the doyen of the American colony." A *Dartmouth Alumni Magazine* article of June 1932 drew a word-picture of him: "Mr. Tuck's figure became a familiar one on the Avenue, as, with his dogs, he took his morning constitutional—square-shouldered, and of strong frame . . . clear, gray-blue eyes with a living light of amiable humor in them; a certain *bonhommie* in his aspect, but a certain dignity, too, that did not encourage easy familiarity . . . essential kindliness, good will, benevolence and friendliness."

In 1898 the Tucks purchased the estate of Vert-Mont, about eight miles from Paris in the commune of Rueil-Malmaison, as a summer home. It was a stunning property, with a three-story chateau and forty-five acres of parks and gardens. At a stone's throw from its gate was Malmaison, with its own beautiful grounds, earlier acquired by the French government to house its Napoleonic collection. On the other side of Vert-Mont was another fine estate; the three properties together had been the original estate of the Empress Josephine. The Tucks had converted some of the larger rooms in Vert-Mont into a museum to house their many Napoleonic treasures (the Tucks were very interested in the arts and acquired many famous paintings and other art objects, both for Vert-Mont and for 82). Later, Tuck purchased the third property, Bois-Préau, and deeded it to France.

Edward Tuck, Financier

In spite of the unhurried life of the Tucks in Paris, Vert-Mont, and Monte Carlo, where they maintained an apartment to escape the summer heat of Paris, Edward had not lost his interest in and ability to understand the business world. In the first place, his and Julia's significant personal holdings of securities required assiduous attention (they were almost all stocks, never bonds; he reportedly told

Château de Bois Préau, *at left,* and Château de Vert-Mont, *bottom.* Courtesy Dartmouth College Library.

Ernest Martin Hopkins, a later Dartmouth president, "I never owned a damn bond in my life, and never expect to"). His real fortune was made in managing these investments; a friend of Beckles Willson said Tuck had "uncanny skill" in picking stocks. Further, Tuck's circle of friends included many of the top leaders of business, connections made during his Munroe service. Tuck kept a running correspondence with most of these people, which was enhanced greatly by his acceptance of a director's position at one of the smaller banks in New York, the Chase National Bank.

Despite Tuck's impeccable connections, he had chosen to be active in just this one business board. It turned out to be very important to his life after his retirement. In 1886, Henry W. Cannon, the shrewd, scholarly man who had just become president of Chase asked Tuck to join its board. Soon the Chase board became even more interesting for Tuck, as Cannon also had persuaded James J. Hill to join it. Hill, of Irish descent, grew up in Canada and later emigrated to St. Paul, Minnesota, where he worked his way up from the bottom in railroading until becoming president of the St. Paul, Minneapolis & Manitoba Railroad (soon to be renamed the famous Great Northern Railroad of the Northwest), with a home office in St. Paul. Hill was a hard-driving taskmaster for the railroads he led, a secretive, proud, and blunt man who brooked no interference but was respected by his railroad associates as a man who knew his operations just as well as he knew the company's financial concerns. Somehow, the abrasive railroader Hill and the courtly Tuck immediately became fast friends, sharing long letters back and forth over many years. There were strong affinities at work here, for railroads and railroad finance seemed particularly to intrigue Tuck, and his holdings were testimony to this.

Albro Martin, Hill's biographer, gave Tuck a distinctly Parisian persona when he dubbed him "charming, witty, and a marvelous raconteur." It was likely this charm and Tuck's European lifestyle that attracted Hill and a fascination with railroading that attracted Tuck. While this long friendship seemed to have only peripheral impact on Hill, who, after all, was involved in a very complex way with the great men of finance in both the United States and Europe, the association held an enormous sway over Tuck. He invested very heavily in Great Northern stock—probably *too* heavily. Martin put it aptly: "Edward Tuck, whether he was staying at his villa in Monte Carlo or in his apartment on the Champs-Elysées, made the Great Northern his chief hobby." Soon Tuck's preoccupation with this one railroad was to have an unexpected but important effect on Dartmouth College.

By political persuasion, Edward Tuck was a Democrat. So too was Henry Cannon, the Chase Bank president, along with a number of other "rich Eastern Democrats" (Albro Martin's description). Tuck was one of the key members of the party. James J. Hill, having met Grover Cleveland in the early 1880s, became his strong supporter after Cleveland had been nominated as the Democratic candidate and had won in the scurrilous presidential campaign of 1884. Hill became a fast friend of Cleveland, even going fishing for bluefish on the presidential yacht when they were running strong off Fire Island.

Tuck was a liberal in terms of his monetary policy, strongly supporting the concept of bimetallism (using gold and silver jointly as a monetary standard, with both constituting legal tender at a predetermined ratio). Cleveland lost a cliff-hanging battle against Benjamin Harrison for the presidency in 1888 but bested Harrison in the following election, in 1892. In the 1896 election, the Democrats were dominated by the bimetallism of the free-silver faction, which called for free and unlimited coinage of silver at a 16:1 ratio with gold. It was during this election that William Jennings Bryan, the Democratic candidate, delivered his eloquent Cross of Gold speech.

At first, Tuck had supported Bryan, but this lasted only until he met Bryan in person. Ernest Martin Hopkins, then secretary of the college, wrote to a Dartmouth colleague: "I presume that you know that Mr. Tuck has always been a bimetallist and that he even swung over to free silver and contributed heavily to the first Bryan campaign—an attitude which he promptly reversed, however, after he met the gentleman, whom he has since always referred to as 'that arch-hypocrite and sanctimonious nincompoop.'" Tuck used still another colorful phrase in a letter to John Bigelow, Tuck's superior at the consulate in Paris in the mid-1860s, calling Bryan "a stuffed prophet." In a subsequent letter to Bigelow he explained his disenchantment: "The first thing which made me suspect Bryan was something that he published in *The Commoner* . . . he said then that it would be the duty of a Democratic President if he came to power to see that 'true friends of the common people' were appointed to the U.S. bench. . . . It seems to me that his occupancy of the Presidential chair would have been . . . a constant menace to capital and to business, which would have destroyed the possibility of a return to confidence and to prosperity." Tuck worried that Bryan was "incapable of understanding the principles of free trade" and that he had advocated bimetallism "simply because he thought it would supply a cheap money and thus please the multitude."

John Bigelow had become one of Tuck's most prolific correspondents, and the two old friends seemed much to enjoy their mutual, sometimes colorful language, especially about politics. Their private, personal musings back and forth give many clues to Edward Tuck's thinking. Bigelow often jested with Tuck about the latter's winter vacation venue; an example: "I sent you a little light reading for your

The Union Pacific had forged the first transcontinental link, with its "golden spike" driven at Promontory Point, Utah, in May 1869. But the Union Pacific was poorly planned, poorly built, and poorly run. For the northern route across the Rocky Mountains, the first candidate to finish the route all the way to the Pacific Coast was the Northern Pacific Railroad. Henry Villard, a devious financier, had outmaneuvered and forced out the Northern Pacific's president, Frederick Billings, and followed this coup with an immediate push to the Pacific Coast, successfully linking Minnesota with the West Coast.

All of this was most disturbing to Tuck's friend, James J. Hill, who had just had his links with the Canadian railroads severed when the latter's majority management insisted on a wholly Canadian route. This forced Hill to think again about the Great Northern's lack of its own routes west. By 1889 he had built a very strong set of connections (east to Buffalo, New York, and westward to Fort Benton, Montana) and immediately planned to breach the Rocky Mountains and the Cascades to reach Oregon. It was to be a daunting route, one that had to be explored quickly before the winter snow set in. Hill actually scouted some of the route himself. He and his colleagues decided on a startling choice. They had the sage advice of a young New Englander, John F. Stevens, who, late in the fall of 1889, alone discovered a new route in northwest Montana, near present-day Glacier National Park. It turned out to be the oft-rumored and long-sought Marias Pass. Amazingly, it was just over five thousand feet in elevation.

Construction began immediately. The construction crews were driven relentlessly, with Hill himself making on-site inspections at frequent intervals. Early in the construction, Hill had had to beat back an end run on Great Northern stock engineered by the redoubtable Villard. When he heard of the threat, Hill went directly to Villard's house in New York City, where the latter was sick abed, and bluntly convinced Villard that he (Hill) and his associates held enough stock to stop *any* raid. Villard backed off at that point.

Worried by this unexpected onslaught, Hill loyalists, particularly those led by two wealthy British holders, Sir George Stephen and Sir Donald Smith, began buying various lots of stray Great Northern

James J. Hill, 1916. Photo: Henry Havelock Pierce, New York; © 1982, 1998 The James J. Hill Group, St. Paul, Minnesota.

stock when they came on the market to prevent any further danger from a sneak attack on the shares. Tuck, too, added to his holdings, which already were quite substantial (by the turn of the century, his twenty-five thousand shares made him the third largest stockholder). By 1893, the new trackage to the West Coast had been finished.

During construction in 1891, Edward and Julia Tuck had made a trip to St. Paul to accompany Hill on one of the latter's endless inspection trips, this one all the way to Montana, then back through Winnipeg on the Canadian route. The trip was marred only by an incident of unpleasantness on the return south from Winnipeg; there was a mixup in arrangements, so the Tucks lost their premium berth and had to take an upper and a lower bunk. There was difficulty with the porter, and Tuck was outraged. A terse message came later from the general manager: "We discharged porter of sleeper St. Hilaire. Mr. Tuck made complaint to me."

During this long stay in the United States, the Tucks had returned to their spacious apartment on West 61st Street in New York City, where they entertained a wide circle of friends, including the Hills,

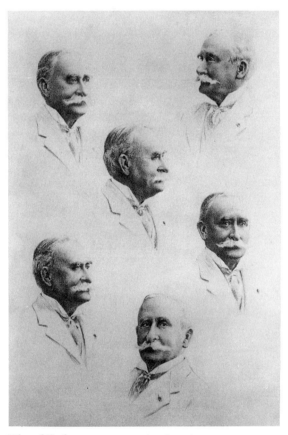

Edward Tuck. Courtesy Dartmouth College Library.

the J. Pierpont Morgans, the George F. Bakers, and the Cannons among the financial people and many artistic, literary, and political celebrities. One of Tuck's biographers noted some of these: "Mrs. Tuck mentions in her diaries the Bigelows, the John Hays, the Whitelaw Reids, and on one or more occasions, Mark Twain, Joseph Jefferson, T. B. Aldrich, W. D. Howells, and Madame Modjeska."

Hill's Great Northern had not been as well received in the East and in European financial quarters as he felt was needed to keep it a credible force in the Northwest. The Northern Pacific had gone into receivership and now was controlled by a group of German financiers. In June 1889, Hill wrote Tuck in Paris, "The more I think it over, the more I am convinced that the thing for us to do is pick the bull by the horns and get control of the N.P."

To do this, the Great Northern needed stronger backing from the wealthy financiers who were dealing widely in railroad stocks. When the Tucks came to America in the winter of 1893–94, Hill made several visits to see them in their New York apartment and urgently petitioned Tuck to prepare a full statement of the current situation of the Great Northern. Tuck agreed and published in the well-known *United States Investor* on January 6, 1894, a thoughtful and compelling argument about the value of the Great Northern as an investment. Tuck pointed out that the railroad owned its own terminals at every point and its elevators, coal mines, and steamers (including "two of the finest passenger boats ever built for inland navigation"). The railroad passed through wheat land, forest, and even the ore-lands of northern Minnesota. Tuck concluded: "[W]ith the road now complete and in the best physical condition, provided with ample equipment of the most modern description, everything paid for and a very large cash surplus in the bank, with no floating debt, the shareholders can await with confidence the development of a profitable traffic from a country which is not surpassed in the United States with its wealth of products from field, forest, mine and sea. . . . Their confidence need not be diminished by the misfortunes of other lines which are geographically parallel but which in all other respects are in no way comparable to the Great Northern." Hill was delighted and telegraphed Tuck (addressing the message to Tuck's Paris cable

Julia Stell Tuck. Courtesy Dartmouth College Library.

address, "Tuckibus"): "Statement couldn't be improved upon. Last sentence masterly."

Hill remained anxious to corner the Northern Pacific, which he felt was one of the culprits in what he called "wild and uncalled-for rate-cutting." Now he moved decisively. Traveling to London in April 1896, Hill made contact with George Stephen (by now Lord Mount Stephen) and Edward Tuck. The three then contacted the representative of the Deutsche Bank, the Berlin group serving as trustees in bankruptcy for the Northern Pacific. The four men met and hammered out what came to be known as "the London Agreement," a plan whereby the Great Northern would take over majority control of the Northern Pacific and in return would guarantee the stressed bonds of the Northern Pacific. The agreement's central proviso covered what Hill and his colleagues really wanted: "The Great Northern Railway Company and the re-organized Northern Pacific Railroad Company shall form a permanent alliance, defensive, and in case of need offensive, with a view of avoiding competition and aggressive policy and of generally protecting the common interests of both companies." Hill exulted to Tuck: "the Great Northern's babe is born, and seems to be a vigorous and healthy infant."

The plan seemed to be further assured of smooth sailing when J. Pierpont Morgan, the head of the great investment banking house carrying his name, joined in the reorganization. Morgan was at the peak of his power at that time and the famous expression "Morganization"—reorganization under the control, indeed, the whip hand of Morgan himself—was soon applicable here. Morgan forced a major role for himself in the appointment of Northern Pacific management, only with the barest, grudging acceptance of Hill, who always preferred to run the show himself. But Hill realized here that he *had* to have Morgan's huge financial resources behind him. A further codicil also became a part of Morgan's plan—a five-year voting trust arrangement that would give Morgan absolute control of any new company for five years. Cannon, the Chase Bank president, advised Hill and Tuck to be wary of the Morgan group: "You will have to be as wise as a serpent and as harmless as a dove with these people."

The entry of J. P. Morgan into the overall railroad picture radically changed much of railroad strategy. Prior to the 1890s the railroad managers' strategic decisions were based more on the moves of their rivals than any logical concentration on the demands for railroad transportation itself. Various formal associations had come into being, but most of these activities—the pools, the drawbacks and rebates—had been outlawed by the Interstate Commerce Act of 1887. This forced the railroaders once again into a pattern of attempted self-sufficiency, which produced more cutthroat competition; bankruptcies threatened, rapidly fueled by the Panic of 1893 and its aftermath.

This panic had begun with the failure of the British banking house of Baring Bros., which soon caused British investors to unload American securities; the resulting drain of gold from the United States brought U.S. reserves below the $100 million mark on April 23. A severe and protracted depression ensued. Between 1894 and 1898, foreclosure sales among the railroads were spread across forty thousand miles of track with a capitalization of over $2.5 billion, making this industry alone responsible for the most massive set of receiverships in American history.

Only the great investment houses, J. P. Morgan and others, had the resources to reorganize these bankrupt companies. Morgan was a high-handed autocrat on setting terms for these reorganizations, so the five-year voting trust he imposed on the Great Northern and the Northern Pacific was in keeping with the general pattern of Morganization. However, the new associations put together by the Morgan and other financial houses failed to include several of the key railroads, and soon the cartels began to disintegrate. This led Morgan and the others in competing investment banking groups to turn toward consolidation as a way out of the difficulty.

In the year 1901, Morgan put together two high-profile consolidations. The first was in the steel industry, where a huge new company, the United States Steel Corporation, became the first billion-dollar corporation. The second involved the Great Northern and the Northern Pacific. By 1898 this reorganization had proved to be reasonably successful. But eliminating the threat of competition from the Northern Pacific still left other interests potentially able to wreak havoc on the Northern Pacific–Great Northern combination. In particular, Edward Harriman's Union Pacific was threatening to shut down some of the Great Northern's access routes into the Portland gateway.

So a fresh consolidation was crafted by Morgan in 1901 with a new holding company, the soon famous Northern Securities Company. One of the great legal and political controversies of this trust-busting period of the federal government then ensued, dragging James J. Hill, its leader, into the maelstrom. Further, Harriman was pursuing a hidden agenda of attack on this new combination, particularly on the Great Northern segment. Edward Tuck was drawn deeply into all of this, with serious implications for his benefactions to Dartmouth College.

All through this period, Hill had antagonized his closest friends by his secretiveness and lack of candor about the Great Northern operations. Even Tuck did not receive communications from Hill quickly enough to consider them timely. For example, after the signing of the London Agreement in 1896, Tuck wrote several months later, "I have never received any copy . . . and as one ought always to put on file a copy of any document of importance which he signs I would be extremely obliged if you would have a copy of it sent to me." Hill had proposed sending several of his children to visit the Tucks, but Tuck had had to cable Hill: "Rooms secured, when do they come?" Receiving no answer, he wrote Hill: "We have been expecting to see or hear from the girls by almost any steamer, but so far have no news about them. Mrs. Tuck has been to the convent, and finds everything ready for them there." He appended a postscript: "I hope you will have sent to me definite figures as to last year's results as soon as you have been able to arrive at them. You know I can never hear too much about the doings and the prospects of the 'old machine' for my own satisfaction."

In the 1896 London Agreement days, when Hill finished the business, he went to Paris and then on to Monte Carlo with his family to visit Tuck. The latter wanted Hill to make more such trips, and the correspondence between the two is filled with Tuck pleadings to know more and urging Hill to visit. In April 1898, Tuck wrote, "Mr. Cannon has called me of your sailing. Who is with you and how long shall you stay? You must not return without having first come to Paris for a few days—when are you likely to come over? Of course I wish very much to see you and have a good Great Northern talk." Hill cabled in return that he could not make the trip to Paris, and Tuck replied, "I will go to London to see you at any time that will suit you best. Of course I cannot miss you entirely. Please let me know when I shall not be in the way, either before or after you go to Berlin and when I can see something of you." Finally, in December of that year, Tuck again renewed his pleadings for a visit: "I am suffering for a good talk with you."

Tuck and Tucker Innovate

Two other persons had been invited by the Edward Tucks to visit them in Paris in that year, 1899—William Jewett Tucker and his wife arrived at 82 in early April. When Tuck had written Tucker the previous fall and intimated that he "wanted to do something for Old Dartmouth," he had ended his letter with the cryptic "I would like very much to see you, for many reasons." Few college presidents could resist a last line like that, and Tucker went.

The year 1899 was the last buildup to what was to be the great Paris Exhibition of 1900. The four friends walked all over the site of the Exposition, by then well in place for its stunning new-century opening just a few months off. There had been and would be several other renowned "world's fairs" around this pivotal change of centuries—the Columbian Exposition in Chicago in 1893, the St. Louis Exposition of 1904. But it was the Paris Exposition that history was subsequently to accord a special role as turning point between the old technology and the new. The historian Henry Adams was there, finding himself (said Patricia O'Toole, in her book *The Five of Hearts,* on the Adams entourage) "mesmerized by the gleaming dynamos in the machine gallery on the Champs de Mars." Adams wrote that he sat by the hour, "watching them run as noiselessly and as smoothly as the planets, and asking them—with infinite courtesy—where in Hell they were going." O'Toole continued: " [I]n their faceless power he read the obituary of his generation." Adams wrote his close friend, John Hay, at that time ambassador to England, "The curious mustiness of decay is already over our youth . . . the period from 1870 to 1900 is closed . . . the period from 1900 to 1930 is in full swing, and gee-wacky! How it is going! It will break its damned neck long before it gets through."

So it was just at this time, in that period of recognition that the Paris Exposition was portending, among other things, a new world with more specialized, more demanding education, that William Jewett

Tucker and Edward Tuck reinstituted their personal friendship. Tucker and Tuck both were thoroughgoing optimists and took a positive view of the new century, opposite to that of Henry Adams, as they now combined to form the Amos Tuck School of Administration and Finance at Dartmouth, the first graduate business school in the country.

They kept no record of the meeting itself, but it must have been an emotional one. Tuck wrote Tucker in London when the latter and his wife were on the way back to the United States, "I am doubly happy, in that it gives me the opportunity of reviving our old friendship of college days, which no later ones can ever replace or make dull, when men are true to themselves and each other." He added, "I am myself very happy in being able to put my shoulder to the wheel in a material way to aid and cheer you in the grand work you are doing." The "material way" was an exciting one: Tuck had agreed to set up an endowment fund booked at $300,000, with transfer of 1,700 shares of Great Northern preferred stock, enough to ensure an income of almost $12,000. A "minor part" was to aid the college library; all the rest was to support instruction both in undergraduate courses and in "post-graduate departments."

The latter part of this designation—the reference to *graduate* education—was a wholly new idea. The full dimensions of this become clear in a remarkable confidential letter written from London by Tucker on April 26, 1899, to Professors James Fairbanks Colby and David C. Wells, two senior members of the Dartmouth faculty and close confidants of Tucker. Colby held a chair as Parker Professor of Law and Political Science, a post established in 1885. Wells had been appointed in that same year as professor of social science; in 1898, his title was changed to professor of sociology. Tucker was not even in a position to disclose to them who the donor was as yet but wanted to alert the two men so that when he returned he could get their advice particularly "in regard to the establishment of a graduate school in Political Science and Finance."

The proposed school was to be at the level of "at least the Thayer School" (Dartmouth's two-year graduate school of engineering), and if an undergraduate degree was not required for entrance, then "a

Julia and Edward Tuck. Courtesy Dartmouth College Library.

high standard in requirements should be demanded." Tucker won-
dered to Colby and Wells: "Would a two-year course be sufficient?"
The subjects contemplated were to include "Modern History, including a study of Modern Diplomacy," a course in the constitutional history of the United States, and work in international law. Further,
there would be a substantial study of administration, to include
governmental, colonial, and municipal aspects. Analysis of the principles of corporations, of advanced economics, and work in customs,
taxation, banking, and currency would be included. The subject of
"ethnology with reference to present race question" was included, a
surprising addition not explored further in Tucker's letter.

The faculty would be made up of three groups: first, professors
from the college in departments related to the subjects noted; second,
two additional professors, one of whom should be a professor of modern history; and third, lecturers on special topics "as in professional
schools." Fellowships would be endowed that would require a year or
two of teaching by the Fellows at Tuck following their graduation.

Then Tucker spelled out some broader concerns. "The main question is the practical outcome of such a school," he began. "What

would become of its graduates? A *few* might find [a] place in the civil or diplomatic service. More might be so qualified for the responsible positions in business (especially in houses that have foreign connections) that openings might be gained for them, though not of course without an apprenticeship." Tucker mused, "I have noticed the growth in numbers of our graduates who go into business. Can we give them a better training, commensurate with *the larger meaning of business* [my emphasis] as it is now understood? Can we enlarge our constituency in this direction?"

Tucker also confided some of his personal concerns. "Incidentally, and yet essentially related to the subject, the question must be faced, can the college expect to maintain itself in its four year course of study without enlarging its immediate connection? Can we hold our men in the future without opening wider ranges of practical study?" A law school "seems impractical," he continued. Most important from a practical standpoint, "is a school like the one outlined . . . called for? Will the Trustees take a strong position in advance for the college, if they establish it, or will they not?"

Similar questions had been posed by Tucker at earlier points in his tenure as president of the college, for he had mused about the practical dimensions of undergraduate education as far back as his inaugural speech in 1893. In that address, widely acclaimed at the time, he stated: "Dartmouth College belongs to a group of foundations, now of historic dignity, which have retained the name, and which continue to exercise the functions of the college, in distinction from the school of technology or the university." But, he queried, "What is the capacity of the College to meet the widening demands of the new education? . . . With special reference to our own environment, what relation may a college sustain to associated institutions without attempting the functions of a university?" The historic college had as its key distinction its homogeneity, but that immediately led to those questions of the "widening demands." The college needed the newer subjects, Tucker maintained, and an education that "enlarges and disciplines the mind irrespective of the after business or profession . . . cannot ignore or omit the training which attends the exact study of nature." Tucker mentioned the Chandler

School at Dartmouth, a technical and scientific program, as well as the Thayer School of Engineering, as examples.

Back in this seminal inauguration speech, Tucker had called attention to a concept that he was to pioneer at the college—"the New Dartmouth." While "the chiefest factor in the new will be the old," Tucker underlined the opportunities available to an institution that saw itself as a college but nevertheless to be attuned to some of the evolving developments in the world of the 1890s. So Tucker had laid the groundwork for a possible new dimension to the associated school concept half a dozen years before he and Edward Tuck had their historic meeting.

Tucker's letter to Colby and Wells was a true masterpiece—from his pen, writing from a London hotel just after he and his wife had left the Tucks, came this innovative outline, not just of a set of courses or an add-on program but of a full-blown graduate school in "political science and finance." Nevertheless, Tucker apparently felt uneasy enough about this concept to lay the matter before these two trusted faculty colleagues and also promised them that before leaving London he would interview a Professor Hewins at the London School of Economics and Political Science, "from whom I may gain some ideas of value."

The Dartmouth reported the Tuckers' return to Boston in mid-May, where they were met by a tugboat in the harbor "loaded with a party of men frantically waving green flags and joining in a hearty 'wah-hoo-wah'" (the hoary "Dartmouth Indian" yell). A few days later, in Hanover, the combined college band and the student body lined up by class to meet the Tuckers.

With Tucker's return to Hanover, face-to-face interchanges among Tucker, Colby, and Wells were frank about both the strengths and potential weaknesses. Colby worried about whether a school "located in this hamlet" could compete with Columbia University's school of political science or the school of diplomacy at Georgetown in Washington. Was there "any *raison d'être* for such a school . . . remote from any commercial or political center?" But Tucker rejected a "go slow" choice. If there were indeed a new field for college men opening up, "can we afford as a College, to not enter and begin to take possession?

If we satisfy ourselves that the opening exists, and that we are capable of entering into it, I think that we must stake something upon the venture. Of course our lines are open for retreat, if that should prove necessary. The chief loss to our venture would be in pride rather than anything of a material or educational character." He concluded, "Of course an infinite amount of money can be spent on the secondary affairs of the College, but I do not like to see so noble a fund as that of Mr. Tuck spent in fragmentary or desultory ways." Finally, a strong, positive consensus evolved, and the men agreed to place the matter before the trustees.

The Graduate School Concept Materializes

By September 1899, Edward Tuck had made his gift a formal one by establishing the Amos Tuck Endowment Fund, which would be in memory of Tuck's father, who had been a graduate of the class of 1835 and a trustee of Dartmouth from 1857 to 1866. Tuck confided to Tucker in a separate letter that he wished the fund to be "a monument to my father's memory in his own state where in his late lifetime he was not appreciated as he should have been. I refer to his public life in which he was the victim of Bill Chandler and his crowd of designing demagogues and pothouse politicians who got control of the Republican party after the war and have held it ever since." In the formal letter, Tuck spelled out that he wished the money to be used to augment the salaries of the president and the faculty and that further amounts would be used for maintenance and increase of the college library. "I can thus encourage and support in a material way," he continued, "the untiring and devoted labors of you, my intimate friend and my only roommate." The matter of the graduate school of business had not yet been agreed to by the trustees, so it was not discussed in Tuck's gift proposal.

Tuck attached one codicil that was to loom large in later events. In tendering his gift of 1,700 shares of preferred stock of the Great Northern Railway, Tuck wrote, "I consider the Great Northern Railway

Preferred Stock one of the most desirable investments in the United States from the point of view of solidity and permanency and I therefore request that no change be made in the investment of the Fund during my lifetime without my approval. It is my desire that this Fund shall be kept intact, and separate and distinct from the general funds of the college."

There was some of the stickler in Tuck, and an amusing example appears in his reply after Tucker sent him a copy of the trustee acceptance of the gift in December 1899: "The resolutions are very gratifying, and I am proud to possess them. They are so well done that I know you wrote them. I do not believe, however, that you attended to the engrossing, for if you had, 'beneficence' would not have been spelt 'beneficience,' as is the case. I think, too, you would have been extravagant enough to put two r's in the word 'embarrassing,' on which Mr. Chase's man economized to the extent of one letter."

The matter of an actual graduate school in administration and finance was sent to the trustees, who formed a special committee to study the matter. At its meeting of January 19, 1900, the Dartmouth Board of Trustees voted to constitute the Amos Tuck School of Administration and Finance. "This school is established in the interest of college graduates," the board resolution began,

> who desire to engage in affairs rather than enter the professions [i.e., law, medicine, and theology]. It is the aim of the school to prepare men in those fundamental principles which determine the conduct of affairs. . . . The attempt will be made to follow the increasing number of college graduates who have in view administrative or financial careers, with a preparation equivalent in its purpose to that obtained in the professional or technical schools. The training of the school is not designed to take the place of an apprenticeship in any given business, but it is believed the same amount of academic training is called for, under the enlarging demands of business, as for the professions or for the productive industries.

The course would cover two years of graduate study; if a student was able to complete courses taken as advanced electives in undergraduate curriculum, he could use these for the first year's work and be given standing in the second year. In other words, the course was adapted particularly to the pattern of a "3/2" arrangement, in which the entire undergraduate and graduate program would be completed in five years. The first-year Tuck courses "shall be largely theoretical," and in the second year "they shall represent the application of theory to particular forms of business as far as practicable." This 3/2 pattern had been adopted early in the Tucker regime by the Thayer School of Engineering (it had been 4/2 from its founding in 1867). Likewise, the medical school had moved from a 3/3 mode before 1890 to three years undergraduate and four years medical. In 1914 a far-reaching change was instituted when the medical training to be undertaken in Hanover was cut from four years to two; Professor Richardson explained, "The compelling reason for this radical change was the scarcity of clinical facilities . . . and the impossibility of meeting the increasing demands for a medical school of high grade without access to a larger number of patients than was available at that time." The remaining two years were taken at another medical school, most often Harvard. In the early 1970s the Dartmouth Medical School returned again to a full four years of medical training in Hanover.

On the basis of this well-understood 3/2 pattern, the new Tuck School now was made official by the trustees. However, there was a lingering concern in that their report failed to mention anything about any degree being given for the work in the new graduate school. Nevertheless, the Tuck School had been launched!

The establishment of the school had an almost instantaneous positive response. In alumni meetings in New York City, in the public press, and all around the campus the excitement generated by a full-fledged graduate program at the college received many accolades. Tuck wrote Tucker in February: "I congratulate you most heartily on the universal approval which your new departure in establishing a School of Administration and Finance has called forth. It will be recognized as filling a gap in modern education which many have grown to be conscious of, but which you are the first to define. . . . You are likely to have imitators, but you will always be honored as the pioneer in this most important and progressive step."

In May 1900 the James J. Hills visited the Tucks in Paris for the Exposition. Edward took it upon himself once again to sing the praises of the railroad magnate to Tucker. In a five-page handwritten letter in that month, he told of how Hill had "made an exact science of railway management. . . . I wish he might explain his methods and system to you, especially his 'Students Class,' where young men are trained in the higher mathematics of railway accounts and taught to calculate the exact cost and efficiency of the average man's labor in every department and of every article that enters into railway construction and operation." Tuck called it "a sort of West Point Academy" in another letter. Hill seemed to be articulating here an excellent example of the burgeoning scientific management movement of the early 1900s, pioneered by F. W. Taylor. (Indeed, the Tuck School in 1911 sponsored a path-breaking major conference on scientific management, with Taylor, Lillian and Frank Gilbreth, Carl Barth, and other luminaries of this field in attendance; the conference was dedicated to Edward Tuck, who had "inspired" it.) Tuck continued on Hill's approach: "In this class only about one in three is found capable of finishing the course, which lasts a year or two, it being a question of the survival of the fittest" (this term once again smacked of social Darwinism). Tuck concluded about Hill: "He is one of the ablest and most remarkable men in America, in every way and as true as steel."

Tuck, after an absence of thirty-five years from any involvement in Dartmouth affairs, now began to evidence some strongly formed opinions about the college that he was not backward about expressing. In August, Tuck wrote Tucker about the college's election of Frank Streeter, a Concord, New Hampshire, lawyer from the class of 1874, as a permanent trustee of the college:

> It has seemed to me for some time that Concord was over-represented on the Board, a feeling which I judge from a circular just received from Manchester is shared in by others. I wish the Board would have a larger representation from other States, men of weight and influence who would be interested and helpful. Perhaps it is harder to find good timber for this purpose than I know; but it seems to be there is more or less wire-pulling among the smaller members of the Alumni to secure

the position of Trustee for men who may not be the most useful to the College. I should have thought that an older graduate, of more than local reputation and influence, could have been found in Massachusetts or further West for the highly honorable position of permanent Trustee, someone who would have added new blood and increased strength to the Board.

By this time, Tucker had sent Tuck a prospectus of the proposed first year of the operation of the Tuck School. Tuck responded with some blunt comments. "If I were to venture a criticism on the preliminary announcement . . . it would be that possibly the courses of instruction as indicated might be considered somewhat complex and overextended. Has the mind of the average college graduate who intends to engage in affairs room for so much, and if pumped into him could he hold and digest it all? This criticism, if justified at all, might be applicable to the paragraphs devoted to Political Science, Sociology, and Demography."

Tuck seemed to be sketching here a rather passive role for a professor in the university, maintaining, "I should say that it was better for the college professor to communicate and discuss principles while abstaining from the application of them to concrete and more or less violently disputed current questions of the day. The student should make the application for himself." Tuck complained also of no mention of the iron and coal industries and worried that "the paragraphs on Law deal with pretty large questions." All in all, Tuck had telegraphed some strong feelings about college education and the position of the educator in the process. He would do so even more pungently later.

The Tuck School's First Years

Remarkably, a full-blown Tuck program *was* in place by the opening of the school year 1900–1901. The formal "Announcement" listed, first, a dozen faculty members, headed by Tucker, Colby, and Wells

Hubbard Hall, the Tuck School's first home, 1901–4.
Courtesy Dartmouth College Library.

with one other senior Dartmouth College faculty member. The remaining were at the assistant professor or instructor level. Clearly, the
most important of these was Frank Haigh Dixon, President Tucker's
son-in-law, who was an assistant professor of economics at the college
and designated as secretary of the new school (in effect, the dean, although that term was not used until 1919). In addition, six nonresident
lecturers for that academic year were listed, giving strong representa-
tion from the business community. John Ordronaux, both a doctor and

a lawyer from New York City, was a lecturer on investments. The railroad industry was represented both in the person of Thomas L. Greene, who managed the Audit Company of New York, lecturing on the principles of railroad and industrial accounting, and James S. Eaton, statistician with the Lehigh Valley Railroad Company. There was a representative from the life insurance industry and from an international trade company in Boston; Robert A. Woods, the protégé of William Jewett Tucker and by this time head of the South End House in Boston, was to lecture on municipal administration.

Just one sentence mentioned the goals of the new endeavor: "The courses of this school are designed to prepare men for those more modern forms of business which have become so exacting as to require the same quality of academic training as the older professions." The remainder of the bulletin laid out the structure of courses required to provide training in a number of separate fields—general mercantile and commercial business, railroad service, insurance, administration, journalism, and training for civic affairs. Students were required to elect eighteen hours each semester, and the specific courses were elaborated in painstaking detail. In the first year, courses in modern history, economics, political science, sociology, language (German, French, and Spanish were offered) and English composition, and speaking were required. There was some interesting terminology in many of these; for example, in the social statistics and applied psychology course, basic information was provided on various vital statistics (birth and death rates, disease and mortality, etc.). "These data are then brought into connection with Crime, Pauperism, and Social Reform. It is the biological side of social life."

The second-year courses were even more detailed in their description and covered the fields of modern history and diplomacy, business organization and management, finance, transportation, accounting, insurance, statistics, law and political science, administration, demography and social institutions, and language; and a thesis "embodying original research and representing work in the field of study . . . may be required." The thesis was to be prepared during the last semester and was to be considered "the equivalent to a course of fifty four [classroom-hour] exercises." (The thesis continued as an

The Tuck School's first class, 1901: *front, from left,* Henry Teague, Walter
Blair; *rear, from left,* Oliver Foster, William Edwards. Courtesy Dartmouth
College Library.

option through the school year 1946–47 but was taken out of the announcements at this point, not to return.)

Four men had completed enough background in the first-year
courses to move directly into the second year in this premier year of
the school. At graduation, the three who had received their bachelor's
degrees the previous year were not given any specific written recognition for their second year of work. The announcement for the following year, 1901–2, was much more substantial and explained this as follows: "The Trustees do not consider it wise at present to confer an
academic degree upon graduates of this School, because no existing
degree adequately expresses the character of the work done, and no
new degree has yet been found which is deemed satisfactory. In lieu
of a degree, the Trustees confer a certificate . . . [giving] evidence of
their fitness to receive it by a final examination or by defense of a thesis. It is felt that this certificate will meet fully the demands of the
students and will prove more acceptable than an academic degree to
the business community."

Not surprisingly, quite the contrary proved to be so; this arrangement would prove most unsatisfactory to the graduates and to the faculty also. So by the third year (1902–3) the announcement stated that the degree of master of science (Tuck School) would be conferred, with the thesis now apparently a required component. This compromise satisfied no one, and the printed announcement contained a small paste-on printed statement as follows: "At a meeting on June 24, 1902, the Trustees of Dartmouth College voted to reconsider their previous action and confer upon graduates of the Tuck School the degree of Master of Commercial Science instead of Master of Science (Tuck School)."

This significant shift in the degree nomenclature came from an extensive discussion among the faculty members sometime just before the June 24 vote of the trustees. Dixon, as secretary of the school, presented a "minute relative to change of degree." He frankly acknowledged that the "Master of Science (Tuck School)" choice "was admittedly only a temporary expedient." Moreover, he pointed out, "it is more than likely that holders of our degree, when using it, will drop the explanatory suffix." In the process, "this brings the degree under the criticism on the one hand of those who maintain that the granting of an academic degree by professional schools is a lowering of academic standards, and on the other of those who desire definiteness in the form of recognition granted to this kind of professional study."

Dixon's memorandum proposed a solution: "The degree should be Master of Commercial Science." He explained, "This form is suggested by degrees now being granted by the State Universities of Ghent and Liege and the Higher Institute of Commerce at Antwerp where Licentiate in the Commercial Sciences is conferred." Given that "the present tendency seems to be to confer at the conclusion of undergraduate work . . . the Degree of Bachelor of Commerce, it might seem logical therefore to adopt the form Master of Commerce. But what would be accepted as natural in a bachelor's degree would appear presumptuous when 'master' is substituted. Furthermore, the abbreviation M.C. would lead to such possible misconception and bantering as to endanger its dignity." On the other hand, he maintained, the Master of Commercial Science "is dignified and academic, is free from the objections noted, and logically follows the baccalaureate in Commerce." Further, it would meet the approval of the business community, or "at any rate, it will not be offensive." The Tuck School, Dixon maintained, was receiving such recognition that "it was not compelled to seek for precedents." He concluded: "It is securing sufficient recognition so that it may safely lead the way in the creation of a second degree in Commerce."

And so the vote went. After the trustees made this decision, they retroactively tendered the degree to the graduates of the first two classes, as well as to the new class. The MCS degree stayed in place until June 1953, when the change to master of business administration—MBA—was made; again, the college offered to change formally the previous MCS diplomas, and numbers of the earlier graduates availed themselves of the offer.

The total number of Tuck graduates was three in 1901, four in 1902, and nine in 1903. While these numbers might have seemed to represent an upward trend, 1904 saw only one graduate!

In the second year of operation, the announcement gave a far more sophisticated description of the aim of the school than in the first year: "It has become evident that business today demands an increase in the number of well-trained and broad-minded men engaged in its service. The intense rivalry which characterizes industrial affairs requires the presence of men of keen insight, solid ability, and the strictest integrity. The analysis of the causes of frequent failures in business leads to the conclusion that these qualities are still too uncommon. In foreign dealings as well as domestic, such men must take the lead if the United States is to hold its own and still further advance its position in the struggle for markets." The statement continued over two full pages, elaborating on the trend toward specialization and drawing analogies between business and the other professions—that "modern forms of business . . . have become so exacting as to require the same quality of academic training as the older professions."

A revealing statement then followed: "The assertion often made that the College unfits men for business is in part true. It has sprung, however, quite as much from the inability or unwillingness of the college graduate to accustom himself quickly to the rigid discipline and the rapid pace of business life, as from the lack of such preparation as is directly applicable to the work in hand." The school had recognized these problems and now rested its plan on a twofold basis. First, business training had to be grounded in a thorough education of the man through the medium of a complete liberal arts undergraduate course: "The sound method seems to be to educate the man first and the business man afterwards." Second, the provision for a graduate year allowed a course of training more rigid than the college "can enforce." Therefore, Tuck would lay quite as much stress on the disciplinary training that would create a proper business attitude as on the educational equipment of the individual. Finally, the school hoped "to so broaden the minds and raise the ideals of its graduates that it will do something to elevate the business community above the plane of mere money-getting." This statement appeared in the announcements over a number of the following years, modified from time to time but containing essentially the same set of precepts.

As the news of the school began to spread, reaction was uniformly positive. Frank Streeter, a newly appointed trustee, put it well in a letter to Tuck: "The establishment of the Tuck School represents a new departure of great consequence and value in education methods . . . it is a pioneer in a new field and has already received general recognition as such, and, if successfully carried on, will stand for . . . a hundred and more years hence." Streeter certainly was prescient when he posited "immense possibilities . . . I am led to believe that we may be dealing with the beginnings of an institution which is to become a great power in the department of *practical* education."

A New Tuck Building

Edward Tuck returned to the United States in 1901. On the way to visiting James J. Hill in Minneapolis and going on to the West Coast in a Hill sleeping car, Tuck stopped in Hanover to visit Tucker at Dartmouth. This was certainly his first visit to Hanover in any sort of official capacity linked to the college administration since he had been a student. It may not have been his first stop in Hanover for other reasons, as he was a native of New Hampshire and may have traveled as far as Exeter and then over to Hanover at one or another time. Once again it was a felicitous meeting for Tuck and Tucker, full of mutual feelings of "good old Dartmouth" (Tuck's way of saying it) and "the New Dartmouth" (Tucker's designation). It was a special recognition that the old aspects of the institution represented by Tucker's and Tuck's days as undergraduates and the new prospects generated for the college as a whole by the adroit and far-thinking Tucker were mutually compatible.

A major practical result of the trip was Edward Tuck's offer to contribute more money to his fund for a new building, to be erected on campus especially for the Tuck School. The business school had started in a renovated faculty home, the Hubbard House. The quarters were not really designed for a major educational effort such as the Tuck School had turned out to be. Edward Tuck recognized this and made a gift at this time of an additional $100,000 for the building. As Tucker put it to Charles P. Chase, the college treasurer, "It won't be necessary to rob our Fund to get our building." Over the next two years a handsome building was planned jointly by the Dartmouth authorities and Edward Tuck. By the time the Tuck School announcement of May 1904, appeared, it included a picture of the almost completed building, on the west side of the College Green (now McNutt Hall).

Edward Tuck's interests in the school reached beyond just the building and the overall finances. Tucker had sent Tuck details of the curriculum, and Tuck wrote to him from Monte Carlo, his family's wintering spot, just before he left for America in February 1901. "I confess that the programme has somewhat terrified me, and I feel disposed to congratulate myself that I am not a pupil, as I doubt if I should be able to get through the course. But this doubtless is because of the immense change that has taken place in all college courses since our day. . . . You have worked out the scheme admirably, and if any changes need be made in the way of simplifying the curriculum they will doubtless suggest themselves with time and experience." Tuck showed himself knowledgeable about business training in the United States, mentioning in this letter both the Wharton School of Finance in Philadelphia (an undergraduate program started in 1881) and also Harvard's programs discussing railway topics (this effort, incidentally, being a result of James J. Hill's interest in that university, a development that clearly unsettled Tuck).

Tuck's interest in and willingness to state opinions on details extended beyond just educational interests. After his visit to Hanover in March 1901, he wrote Tucker: "I hear from time to time complaints of the discreditable carriage accommodations from the station to the town, and of the poor hotel in Hanover. I hope that for the credit of the College these minor matters are having some attention and will be rectified as far as possible, for they cause many people to carry away bad impressions." Indeed, Tuck was voracious for details and more than once gently needled Tucker to send various Dartmouth materials more promptly.

At the college graduation exercises in June 1903, Edward Tuck was given an honorary degree of doctor of laws. After their strenuous visit to the United States in 1901, going all the way to Montana with Hill, Edward and Julia were not up to a further trip so soon, and the notification of the degree came in a letter from Tucker in late June. "The honor was too great for the man," Tuck remonstrated to Tucker, "especially when I see my name coupled with such distinguished ones as those of Captain Mahan and Professor Young. I recognize in the language in which the degree is conferred your own peculiar felicity of expression and delicate sentiments." Clearly, Tuck was thrilled with the honor.

Meanwhile, the construction of the new Tuck building proceeded apace. Suddenly, however, the fortunes of the college took a sickening change for the worse: a startling event occurred that affected many of Tuck's plans for the school. On February 18, 1904, beloved Dartmouth Hall, a historic feature on the east side of the green since 1784, caught fire. The interior was quickly gutted, with damage also to the exterior—"totally destroyed," said the minutes of the trustees. It was a shattering loss to the college. The trustees met two days later and the minutes captured the shock:

Dartmouth Hall is destroyed, February 18, 1904. Courtesy Dartmouth College Library.

Dartmouth Hall served the College for nearly a century and a quarter by supplying rooms for students and for recitations, and during a large part of the period, an assembly room for the devotional and other general exercises of the College. Though its style of architecture was very plain, its proportions and location were such that, with its beautiful belfry, it was a very pleasing building to look upon. But its utility and beauty were insignificant when compared with the memories that clustered about it. It entered into, and became a part of the lives of the thousands of men who have gone out from the College during these years. It embodied almost from the first the traditions of the College and stood to the last as the embodiment of the active life of the College. In the words of the President, when he met the students a few hours after the fire, "Dartmouth Hall is now a memory, but the spirit which inspired it remains untouched and will rise to face the future years."

Tucker cabled "Tuckibus," and Tuck responded immediately. "A great misfortune," Tuck stated, "the burning of Old Dartmouth." He continued with his concerns about how funds would be obtained for rebuilding. Over lunch on the day they first met, the trustees had talked of the rebuilding and had made an instant decision—that immediate steps would be taken "to raise funds sufficient to reproduce, in more permanent form, Dartmouth Hall upon the present site, and to provide for those uses which have stood in the working life of the College." The trustees judged that a sum of $250,000 would be required to do that. Various members of the board made immediate plans to fan out among alumni groups to make this case for the funds.

Edward Tuck worried: "I was thinking that this would necessarily modify very much the plan suggested in your letter of appealing for yearly subscriptions to the graduates . . . and would lead you to make a larger and more comprehensive programme. . . . With this conviction on my mind, your cable just received indicates that my anticipations were correct, the information just received informing me that there is already a movement among the alumni to raise $250,000." Tuck had been skeptical of the Dartmouth alumni's willingness to back up good feelings with cash support and reiterated that "the present would seem to be a most opportune occasion to materialize into substantial pecuniary aid some of the sentimental and oratorical, though nonetheless genuine, enthusiasm which has been awakened among the graduates all over the country."

Teddy Roosevelt Intrudes

Once again, the overarching impact of the Great Northern railroad on Edward Tuck's fortunes came into play. A national tragedy now profoundly influenced this course of events: on September 6, 1901, President William McKinley, in the first year of his second term, was killed by an assassin, and Theodore Roosevelt became president. In his first message to Congress in December of that year, Roosevelt recommended rigorous action to abolish abuses by trusts and combines. When Congress vacillated, Roosevelt's first act was to resolutely file suit in February 1902 for the dissolution of the Northern Securities Company, the holding company chartered by the Hill forces to hold the stock of both the Great Northern and the Northern Pacific (and control of the Burlington Railroad). Roosevelt exhorted, "We do not wish to destroy corporations but we do wish to make them subserve the public good."

Against the advice of J. P. Morgan, Hill decided to fight the government's case with his strongest possible defenses. Many cable messages in a code devised by Hill went back and forth between Hill and Tuck, concocting various Hill strategies. Here is one; the words, when translated, report actual quarterly earnings and calculate how much information to withhold and how much to make public:

Tuckibus, Paris

Renown November winker enshade enrapt/ wolf about same/ wigwam ensafe enmity/ total enshroud will publish for winker enpoison less

Hillrail

J. P. Morgan had his own private agenda: he wanted to preserve his United States Steel merger and other railroad consolidations he had engineered. Roosevelt, too, had proceeded with the Northern Securities prosecution without the backing of his key colleagues, particularly that of Mark Hanna, the hardheaded political boss who had supported Roosevelt. So the battle was joined between the two implacable men, Roosevelt and Hill. Teddy left no doubt as to his motives of rigorous trust-busting when he told western author Hamlin Garland later in the spring of that year, "I have ordered taken down the fences of a very great and very arrogant corporation."

This battle took its toll on the Northern Securities shareholders' stock values, Dartmouth included (for its Great Northern shares had been converted to the Northern Securities shares). The fundamentals of the Great Northern and Northern Pacific properties still seemed positive, however. To Hill's dismay, in April 1903 the circuit court in Minnesota that was hearing the case ruled unanimously against Northern Securities and ordered its dissolution. Tuck, in Paris, cabled Hill in his uniformly optimistic mode: "Friends here generally unterrified. Will await with confidence ultimate solution."

As the case was to be the first test of the Sherman Antitrust Law of 1890, it went immediately to the Supreme Court. Tuck wrote Hill, "The Supreme Court will be surrounded in Washington by a different atmosphere than that existing in St. Paul. It will hear less of the un-reasoning clamour of the masses against capital, and will appreciate more the necessity of protecting investments." But optimism could not swing the result. In March 1904, the Court made its ruling: in a split decision, 5 to 4, it upheld the government's case.

The ruling was made just a few weeks after the Dartmouth Hall fire, and Tuck reported to Tucker, in the same letter in which he pledged $10,000 toward the $250,000 goal to rebuild, "this unfortu-nate and interminable Northern Securities litigation has acted as a damper upon everything and tends to diminish any philanthropic tendencies among my particular friends." In several letters during this event-filled spring, Tuck emphasized that all Dartmouth alumni had to put "our shoulders to the wheel," but, at least among share-holders owning Northern Securities, Tuck's urgings did not produce results.

Now the Court ordered the Northern Securities Company to di-vest itself of all its railroad stock, and Hill forthwith instituted a plan providing that its assets would be redistributed pro rata, so that each shareholder in the Northern Securities Company received equal parts of Northern Pacific and Great Northern stock regardless of what his original holdings had been, thus preserving the control as before. Immediately, Edward Harriman saw his chance to attain his long-sought objective of control of the Northern Pacific and peti-tioned the Court to set aside the pro rata basis and attempt to recon-struct each person's original holdings from the two railroad compa-nies. If this contention were to be adopted, Harriman thought, it would give him control of the Northern Pacific because at this time he had a clear majority of its stock. Fortunately for Hill, the Court ruled against the Harriman claim. At this point, Harriman gave up his

Tuck himself, has remained throughout all of the school's building changes over the years and is still there today to state the principles under which Tuck endowed the school. It reads as follows:

> In the conduct of the School to which you have done my father's memory the honor of attaching his name, I trust that certain elementary but vital principles, on which he greatly dealt in his advice to young men, whether entering upon a professional or business career, may not be lost sight of in the variety of technical subjects of which the regular curriculum is composed. Briefly, these principles or maxims are these: absolute devotion to the career which one selects, and to the interests of one's superior officers or employers; the desire and determination to do more rather than less than one's required duties; perfect accuracy and promptness in all undertakings, and absence from one's vocabulary of the word "forget"; never to vary a hair's breadth from the truth nor from the path of strictest honesty and honor, with perfect confidence in the wisdom of doing right as a surest means of achieving success. To the maxim that honesty is the best policy should be added another: that altruism is the highest and best form of egoism, as a principle of conduct to be followed by those who strive for success and happiness in public or business relations as well as in those of private life.

Today there likely would be more than a few caveats on this wording. For example, that term "absolute" telegraphs too much of hierarchical rigidity and authoritarianism, and modern decision analysis has redefined with more realism some of the concepts of "perfect accuracy." Still, one hopes that the essence of Edward Tuck's words ring as true today as in 1904, to become, as well a contemporary statement of many of Tuck School's basic values.

Tuck had made an additional grant of $75,000 in November 1904 to provide for equipping and maintaining the new Tuck building. In April 1905, he also sent his subscription for the Dartmouth Hall reconstruction and wrote Tucker: "You will probably be glad to see the money in the locker in view of the completion of the building this year, which I understand you expect." The new building itself, with

Final construction phase for the Tuck School, May 1904. Courtesy Dartmouth College Library.

"Tuck School" carved over its front door, was spacious and commodious. Located on the West Row, next to today's Parkhurst Hall, in a preeminent position facing Dartmouth Hall across the green, it became an important feature of the central Dartmouth campus. (The building was changed to McNutt when the Tuck School moved in 1930.) The building was three stories high, the main portion being one hundred by fifty feet, with an addition at the rear of sixty by forty feet at the same height as the main building. On the first floor were the administrative and instructors' offices, several "recitation" (teaching) rooms, and a lecture hall, equipped with "projecting and reflecting apparatus" and seating 278 persons—one of the prized lecture halls on campus in those earlier years. The second floor housed more recitation rooms and offices, as well as a "seminary room" (the extra *y* was unintentional, not to imply a theological seminary!). The specialized business library was on this floor, too. (The main library, across the green at Wilson Hall, held the college collections.) An accounting room with the then state-of-the-art calculating machines completed the floor. The third floor had a museum, containing exhibits of domestic industries (e.g., raw material and products, slides, photographs, maps and other "illustrative matter"). All in all, the school had taken a quantum leap in modernization with its new building.

Curriculum Development

The 1904–5 announcement was a more polished version overall. An initial section on the aims of the school had undergone some substantial modification; now the focus on general management was more direct, as was the desire to "develop broadness of view, independence of thought, and a spirit for business activity." This, it was hoped, would "produce men a large percent of whom, beginning at the bottom, would soon show such a capacity for taking responsibility as would cause them to be rapidly advanced out of the routine positions into those of the higher class. It is not unreasonable to suppose, also, that under modern business conditions future managers and proprietors are likely to come from this class."

General management as a defining predominant thread for the Tuck School, one that has been so strongly evident to the present, was at that time made part of an intensive three-year study by the faculty, looking toward the development of a centralizing course in organization for the school. The new course was first offered in the 1913–14 academic year and soon came to include a "clinic" component involving work with local New Hampshire and Vermont businesses and chambers of commerce. A separate supplement of the announcement, "The Training of Commercial Executives," published in April 1916, defined this in detail.

The 1904–5 curriculum also went through a refining process. A link with Thayer School evolved, and there was even a focus on preparing some of the students for going "to the newer and less developed countries" (the phrase "less developed" was a modern term ahead of its time). A separate paragraph spoke briefly of adapting the

The Dartmouth College class of 1902 graduation, on the way to the Bema (a Dartmouth open-air amphitheater). Courtesy Dartmouth College Library.

program to those entering journalism, and there was a more extensive section emphasizing some students' "preparation for teaching commercial subjects." Tuck School was to join with the Department of Pedagogy at the college to offer a course of study designed to prepare men for eventual work in "academies and high schools."

The set of courses in the remainder of the curriculum was essentially that featured in the earlier announcement; now specific professors were assigned to each course area, and the student could identify who his professor would be. Railroad service continued to be a major focus, and sociology and political science still comprised a major segment of the first-year work. Today's highly important marketing component of graduate business schools was only incompletely met at that time, as a subhead of "Commerce and Industry"; the key course was "mechanisms of trade." A modern language was still a requirement throughout the first year of the program, with French, German, and Spanish being available. The thesis at the end was a segment of the total experience, one that remained for many years into the future.

Tuck School's 1903 graduating class: front, from left, Albert Dalrymple,
Irving French, Ralph Carleton, Amos Fitzgerald, Philip Brown; *rear, from
left*, Percy Dorr, Christopher Fullington, Raymond Paine, James Drake.
Courtesy Dartmouth College Library.

The section in the announcement on "expenses" noted that the
tuition was still $100, and the estimate of total expenses had not
changed from that first year: $275–$550 per year. Frank H. Dixon, the
economics professor, had been the head of the Tuck School for the
first three years, with the title of secretary. With the 1904–5 announcement, a new name entered the picture with the appointment
of Harlow S. Person as the leader, still with the title of secretary. A
later head of the school, William R. Gray, who first held the title of
dean (in 1919) had just joined the faculty. He was instructor in accounting and mathematics, having graduated from Dartmouth College in 1904 and obtained his MCS degree from Tuck School in 1905.

Edward Tuck wrote Tucker in December 1904 of his pleasure at
the progress of the school: "I am pleased that you are so well satisfied
now with the composition of the faculty at the Tuck School. Young
men are coming to the front these days as never before in all the active pursuits of life. It is a rule on the Great Northern Railroad to
take no new employees over thirty years of age."

However, a letter from Tuck to Tucker later in that year communi-
cated substantial unease about the college as a whole.

In your day and mine there was certainly a good deal of poor material sent to college and many men received the benefit of the course who would have done better in other avocations that do not need a college education. I remember that my classmate Clark, who wrote the Chronicles for class-day, remarked that the country towns of New England had sent to our class the flower of their youth to become college bred. This was a very good pun but not strictly in accordance with the facts. Oftentimes, instead of being the flower it was the barren stock. For this reason, I have sometimes queried whether the enormous increase in college classes all over the country of late has not to some extent involved a waste of educational effort upon young men who might better go to work in some more humble calling than the professions. It is true of course that men are supposed to be educating themselves nowadays in much larger numbers than ever before for business occupations. I do not remember that in our day any student expected to go outside of the three so-called learned professions. However, I have no doubt that as Dartmouth grows in numbers you will seek also as far as possible to improve the quality with the increasing quantity. I do not know what average proportion of the applicants to college is received or what rejected. There can be no doubt but what you are right in feeling that the College must keep up with the procession as it is moving all over the country, both in growth and activity.

The Dixon Incident: Academic Freedom

With the high level of hostile rhetoric against the railroads in President Roosevelt's second term, Edward Tuck's defensiveness about the attacks against that industry increased. Along with this, Tuck seemed more strident in his antagonism toward Roosevelt. He certainly was not alone there!

But there were other views. When Frank Dixon gave up his administrative position in favor of Harlow Person, he was advanced to full professor in the Economics Department and began to concentrate

An informal group of Tuck students and undergraduate friends, c. 1903.
Courtesy Dartmouth College Library.

both his teaching and his research on transportation. It was natural
that he should have the railroads as one of his central interests. Back
in the summer of 1902, Tucker had mentioned Dixon's interest to
Tuck, and the latter replied, "You speak, by the way, of Professor
Dixon being already familiar with the methods of the management of
the Great Northern Railroad. I hope this covers a knowledge concerning Mr. Hill's Railroad School for young men, and of the remarkable tables of comparative statistics . . . which were first devised by
Mr. Hill . . . and which have been more or less copied by the best
managed railway companies in the country." Tuck continued with his
often effusive praise of Hill: "[He] has made an exact science of railway accounting as regards both the management and construction. . . . The methods which he first introduced, and are now being
generally adopted, are accountable to a considerable extent for the
present unexampled prosperity of our railroads generally."
    Dixon asked Tucker to query Tuck about an interview with Great

Northern management. Tuck accommodated him, writing to Louis Hill, the vice-president son of James J. Hill (and Hill's choice as his successor). Dixon subsequently visited the Great Northern home offices in St. Paul. In December 1905, Dixon published his first major article on his research, entitled "President Roosevelt's Railroad Policy." It appeared in a new Dartmouth publication, *The Dartmouth Bi-Monthly* (later renamed the *Dartmouth Alumni Magazine*), just in its second issue. Running over eight pages, it was a lengthy piece, a tightly knit analytical effort. His approach was reasoned, and the rhetoric was in no way excessive. But Dixon left no doubt about his strong support of Roosevelt's policies vis-à-vis the railroads. It was an issue of great importance to the country, Dixon began. "None but a Robinson Crusoe can escape, . . . [it] touches people so personally . . . so universally." He first sketched the historical buildup, both the original passage of the Interstate Commerce Act of 1887 and the subsequent difficulties that the Interstate Commerce Commission had in enforcing the original intent. The courts, under pressure from the railroads, had narrowed the scope of the ICC, delimiting the commission in three important respects: (1) it could not fix a "reasonable rate," (2) it could

James J. Hill on rear platform of train, Litchfield, Minnesota, 1912. Photo © 1982, 1998 The James J. Hill Group, St. Paul, Minnesota.

not equalize the transportation conditions for different producing sections and markets through enforcement of the long haul/short haul clause, and (3) the railroads were not required to present a complete case in an ICC hearing but could wait until the court case to make its arguments. Pooling was now severely constrained, but many other devices were still being used by the railroads to continue their special rates to favored shippers. Some of the ICC difficulties were remedied in legislation passed in 1903. But the ICC still had no ability to define and then to set "reasonable" rates. It was this latter concern that was being addressed by Roosevelt at this particular time.

At the end of the article, Dixon also briefly addressed the safety of railroad travel. Inasmuch as "many railroad officials will consider the interest of the public in the matter of safety only when compelled to do so by the force of legislative decree," he wrote, "their great achievements do not warrant their disregarding the appalling figures of railroad accidents . . . or in refusing to recognize their paramount obligation as public servants."

Of course, Edward Tuck was one of the first to see Dixon's article, and the whole piece was anathema to him. The railroad industry had been under attack for more than twenty-five years; now, a sharply worded, detailed attack had taken place in a publication of his beloved Dartmouth College. He immediately wrote Tucker. The letter itself is no longer extant, but Tucker's reply (of February 26, 1906) left no doubt about both Tuck's feelings and Tucker's in response. In the context of the close relationship between the two old friends and the obvious financial impact on the college, Tucker's letter in return was blunt and to the point, a remarkable exposition on the concept of academic freedom. It read in part as follows:

My dear Tuck:

I understand your feeling in regard to any discussion adverse to the railroads on the Rate Bill, but I think that you have a mistaken view in regard to the policy of such a discussion on the part of Economic men [i.e., professors of economics]. The fact is that the habit of college men has changed greatly since you knew more directly about the relations of academic men to the public and to public questions.

A great many of the leaders in the daily press, bearing upon political questions, are written by college professors. In regard to this particular measure, it was the large question for discussion at the recent meeting of the Economic men in Baltimore [the annual convention of the American Economics Association], and the fact of the discussion awakened no comment whatsoever. President Hadley of Yale, formerly in the Chair of Economics, has just written an article on the subject; also Professor Ripley of Harvard has published two articles in the *Atlantic Monthly*; also, Professor Myers of Chicago University, and another Professor Myers of Wisconsin University have written, one for and the other against the bill. In fact, the discussion of this subject is so general among academic men that it would be considered a very great academic impropriety to put a veto on any man's utterances on this or any like subject.

Professor Dixon wrote the article for *The Dartmouth Bi-Monthly* in response to a special request from the editor, who is soliciting articles from the Faculty and Alumni on subjects of public interest on which they may be informed. I happen to know that Professor Dixon's personal opinions, as well as his sympathies, were the other way, but that more recent investigation has led him to modify his views.

In regard to Mr. Roosevelt's attitude on the railroad question, and one or two others of like nature, I think that some of the shrewdest politicians in the Republican party believe that, through this action, he is the breakwater against Bryanism. I had quite a talk in the early winter with Luther Little, secretary of the Republican Club in New York, one of our graduates in the early 1880s and one of the keenest observers we have among our younger political men. I think that he feels very strongly that the Republican Party is liable to a serious overturn unless it makes some concession to public demands. Mr. Roosevelt is, as everybody knows, a man of mixed characteristics, but I think he has a considerable gift of interpretation. He is really a conservative in opinion though a radical in action.

I shall write you much more fully on some other matters before long. I write in this matter in reply to yours of January 22, in order that you may see something of the conditions of academic and political life as they are running together in the country at present.

Tucker ended with some conciliatory words about the Great Northern and James J. Hill, closing: "The Hill management comes nearest to an ideal management of corporate properties of any management within my knowledge."

Edward Tuck, unwilling to give an inch, wrote three weeks later to Tucker:

> You say you "understand my feeling in regard to any discussion adverse to the railroads on the Rate Bill, but that I have a mistaken view in regard to the policy of such a discussion on the part of Economic men." I suppose you must mean that you understand my feeling in the matter because of the effect such a bill might have on my private interests. Your seeming suspicion is not justified, my only railroad interests being in Mr. Hill's properties and, as he says, the country will be covered with railroad corpses long before the commission gets down to us. . . . I am opposed to the Bill wanted by Roosevelt because as President Hadley says, "It is based on bad principles," and would, I believe, inevitably arrest the development of many of the most important interests of the country, railroads and others, and in the end have to be repealed as was the similar Granger legislation of 30 years ago. I will not argue this with you, however, but merely refer you to the enclosed editorial from a recent *New York Times*, which expresses my own views much better than I could.

Tuck then commented about Tucker's view of Roosevelt:

> That "considerable gift of interpretation" which you euphemistically attribute to him caused him to see that to attack the Tariff would mean a cessation of the money contributions necessary to perpetuate Republican rule, while an attack on the Railroads would satisfy the Populistic clamour against corporations and not be open to the same pecuniary consequences. The rantings of patriots like Bill Chandler and Bourke Cochran help the President by exciting the public regarding evils which are mostly imaginary and by distracting attention from the Tariff, although the abuses and grievances under the latter are a hundred fold greater than they are in the railroad field.

I am surprised that you should appear to justify the adoption by the Republicans, as "breakwater against Bryanism," of what is actually the most populistic of Bryan's doctrines. I do not see that Republican Bryanism is any better for the country than Democratic Bryanism. I think in any case it is a mistake of partisan zeal on the part of the College presidents and "Economic men" to take up the public defense in the interests of a political party of a doctrine so questionable as to call forth a denunciation like that of Senator Foraker which I believe expresses the views of the vast majority of property owners in the United States. Regardless of the "great academic impropriety" of putting a veto on any man's utterances on this subject to which you call my attention, I confess to a very great regret that such a doctrine should be advocated as I understand it has been in a school to which my father's name is attached.

At the end of the letter, Tuck added in his own handwriting, "Excuse me for expressing my opinion with perfect plainness but as between old friends I believe it is always best." Still not satisfied that he had made his message completely clear, Tuck appended a P.S., again in his own handwriting: "I am mortified that the official sentiment of Dartmouth College should go out of its way to take sides with Roosevelt on this question, against the judgment of our most enlightened and independent press and of our ablest and most disinterested businessmen. I believe the time will come when you all will regret it yourself."

Tucker waited several months before replying to this unexpected letter. Tucker's letter was a masterpiece. It first talked of the Tuck School in glowing terms: "I think that among the different and perhaps unrelated influences which are at work to build up the College, none is more marked, at present, than the Tuck School idea. Men of information and intelligence, who are concerned with education and are interested in it, and a great many businessmen are as I have before said to you, sending their sons to Dartmouth because Dartmouth has recognized and embodied the idea of giving to certain businesses professional rank, provided the requisite academic training can be given."

Then there were positive words for the Great Northern and, particularly, for its president: "I am more and more impressed with the essential greatness of Mr. Hill. I think that he is one of the few very strong men now in command of the resources of the country. I think that his integrity is one source of his greatness. To contrast his methods and aims with those of certain promoters keeps one's faith in human nature, when entrusted with power."

Tucker then turned to the issues that so manifestly disturbed Tuck, raised in his previous letter:

> You are, of course, perfectly aware of the social turmoil we are passing through in this country, though I doubt if you can feel the full force of it. The questions, for the time being before us, are no longer political, but social. We are in danger of a class war, partly through the indifference and thoughtless behavior of some men of financial power and partly through the unscrupulous arts of some demagogues in arousing popular prejudice. . . . Men unused to politics may not always act wisely, but their interest, at the present time, is a healthy sign. . . . Our College community represents perhaps a hundred men of various training and their different localities. Of course, they do not think alike on subjects, religious, political, or even educational, but I think that in common with most academic men of today, they are trying to act honestly and with discrimination. . . . I understand perfectly the vexations of a man like Mr. Hill who knows that his intentions are right, and for that matter his schemes also. . . . The laws are not made for the righteous. There are men whose ambitions and methods must in some way come under responsible review, or else we shall have trouble. One effect of recent discussions is that intelligent men amongst us are learning to discriminate, and have faith enough in the people at large to believe that they too, in time, will discriminate.

There the matter rested. The two friends had been uncommonly blunt with each other, yet there seemed to be no longer-term hurt. It is clear from this exchange and from others in the Tuck papers, that Tuck was not used to having anyone challenge him in his thinking, and he seemed often to brook no criticism. That there was no animosity resulting from this remarkable exchange of letters is testimony to the quality of both men.

Tuck was not finished, however. Dixon had gone on to write a strong article in the *Atlantic Monthly* of May 1907, with considerable similarity to the one in *The Dartmouth Bi-Monthly.* It was addressed particularly to the railroads' accident records. Although we do not have any record of the response of the two Hills, James J. and son Louis, it seems clear from another Tuck letter that they had not only taken issue with Dixon on the tenor of his article but also felt that Dixon had unfairly used materials from the Great Northern in the article. (In truth, there was no mention whatsoever of the Great Northern in either of the two articles.) Dixon wrote a letter to Tuck in May 1907, denying that there was any possible inference that any part of the article referred specifically to the Great Northern or that it even alluded to the tales that Dixon had learned while visiting that company's headquarters.

Tuck now replied to Dixon about the latter's response to the Hills:

This letter confirmed the view I had taken in my letter to Louis Hill . . . that I had found nothing in your article published in the *Atlantic Monthly* which indicated that you had used in its preparation information gained from the Great Northern office. But evidently Mr. Fairington and Mr. Louis Hill had read between the lines of your article and detected the hostile trend of your mind towards transportation corporations generally, which your later articles have made manifest. I have never said nor thought that you had misused my confidence in connection with the information gained from the Great Northern Railway, but I confess to mortification for having recommended to the courtesies of the Company one who has gone beyond the sphere of his professional duties to contribute his small share in fanning the flames of that popular indiscriminate persecution of American Railways which has resulted in the present destruction of confidence in what have heretofore been considered our best investment securities and consequent grave material injury to the most important interests of the country, the end of which is not yet.

It is not hard to imagine the effect on a professor of receiving such a letter from a prominent benefactor of the institution, and we are forced to the conclusion that Edward Tuck, like all of us, was human and subject to excesses in response when faced with attacks on institutions that he valued highly.

Tuck sent a copy of his letter to Dixon to Benjamin A. Kimball, the Concord lawyer and one of the key Dartmouth trustees. Kimball responded: "Yours of June 6th enclosing copy of letter to Professor Dixon was received, and certainly interests me very much. I read it to Mr. Tuttle last week. He was very much pleased at the strong, logical and emphatic way in which you stated the facts. It is very good." This last sentence did seem to put Kimball squarely in Tuck's corner.

The Panic of 1907: Tuck Reacts

The country's stock markets had dropped early in 1907, and business failures began to mushroom by the middle of the year. Then came a significant tightening of credit and resulting unemployment. Edward Tuck, from his vantage point in Paris, now found again that being so far away was a disadvantage—he did not know what was happening and, particularly, could not get much information from Hill about the Great Northern properties. John Bigelow agreed that "Hill cultivates the character of a Sphinx and lets nobody know what he is going to do for us while making us all the time indulge in hopes that he means to do great things for us."

Tuck now decided to renew contact with his old friend George F. Baker, who at this point had become one of the most prominent bankers in the country as president of the First National Bank of New York (today's Citicorp). He began his first letter to Baker,

> You once said that you had thought occasionally of writing me about matters of mutual interest to us. I feel now that I am more in the dark than I have ever been before regarding the future of our favorite prop-

erties. Is the Great Northern to buy out the Northern Pacific interest
in the Burlington, or is it not? I have heard from London that J. J. Hill
says it cannot be done and yet the quotations would indicate that an
extra dividend was coming on the old N.P. stock. If the Great Northern does buy the N.P. interest, is there any likelihood of the G.N.
shareholders getting a distribution of new shares or something which
will represent the value of the Burlington equity to them? Are the politicians going to allow us ever to get what properly and honestly belongs to us? Do the Ore Properties look to you as promising an investment as they have appeared to be in Mr. Hill's estimation? Are we
likely to get a dividend on them this year? And is there no fear of hostile legislation which may destroy by taxation a large part of the value
or income of the properties? Do you feel hopeful that the market will
be able to absorb the enormous allotments of new stock coming upon
us during the next 20 months without some further recession in
prices? Do you think it prudent and wise for me to carry along a considerable portion of my installments on time money rather than to sell
the new stock at the ruinous prices which are now prevailing?

Baker immediately sent a long, handwritten response and tried to
address each of Tuck's questions. Urging him to "stand pat on your
installments," Baker attempted to reassure Tuck about the overall situation: "We have seen the worst . . . money is working easier."

By September, Tuck again wrote Baker: "Doubtless Mr. Hill
thought when he announced publicly that 7 percent was his dividend
limit [that] his self denial and liberality towards the public would be
properly appreciated by them but, as we all know, while he has done
more for the North West than any other man living he has got only
persecution instead of thanks for it. As our age and experience grow,
I think we are all getting more and more to be of the opinion of Com-
modore Vanderbilt regarding the good public expressed so tersely
many years ago." Vanderbilt's famous statement was "the public be
damned."

On October 22 one of the financial houses of New York City, the
Knickerbocker Trust Company, suspended, and a true panic now
overwhelmed everyone. Baker and Tuck had gone through the panic

of 1873 together, when another important financial house, Jay Cooke
& Co., went bankrupt. Tuck wrote Baker of his personal dilemma,
"As I have some large loans maturing later on, I made up my mind I
ought to close all outstanding accounts and put myself in cash so as
to be prepared to meet my loans in case they were not renewable. I
think this is the first time in 25 years that I have not an account in
any broker's office. Of course I did not foresee the failure of the
Knickerbocker Trust Company."

But there was something more serious in this letter that Tuck felt
a compulsion to air. A few weeks earlier, he had allowed himself to
engage in some loose talk with his nephew Amos Tuck French, an
impetuosity quite unlike him:

> Amos French writes me that he read to you my letter to him in regard
> to the 1 percent dividend on Ore Stock and that you said that it was
> unfair for me to say that insiders had sold. I have just been looking
> over the copy of the letter, which I wrote hastily, and I fully agree with
> you that it was unfair for me to say so in the bold and careless way in
> which I did, for it seemed to mean more than I intended. I have never
> thought for an instant that any of my immediate friends had sold the
> stock, and I hope you did not imagine I meant them. I know Mr. Hill
> only recently has said this stock will some day surprise people by its
> dividends, and we all know that Mr. Hill never says anything that he
> does not believe in which is not in the end justified. I referred in my
> mind to certain reports which had come to me from St. Paul, to the
> effect that those nearest the property there did not share in Mr. Hill's
> optimistic views and said the stock was not worth over 50 and had
> sold their stock accordingly. . . . It was somewhat under this influence
> that I wrote Amos and expressed myself too carelessly. I should be
> very sorry if you thought me capable of believing that any of our im-
> mediate party had sold out on the others.

Edward Tuck probably was indiscreet in having said this to his
nephew, but the fact remained that some of the larger shareholders
thought to be central to and dependable for the Great Northern and
its ore properties had indeed sold out without notifying the others.

This particular incident passed without further comments, but the possibility was always present that individual shareholders would privately sell their shares and thus undercut the company's strength in the financial markets. Tuck was going to have a further example of this at a later point, one that would cause him much concern and grief. With the consternation throughout the country at the Knickerbocker suspension, J. Pierpont Morgan and other financial leaders intervened and steadied the market. They finally were able to restore a modicum of confidence by advancing massive loans to businesses (their action coining the term "banker's panic"). The situation moderated as the new year began and turned out to be primarily a severe but short-term liquidity squeeze; it was not followed by depression, as had happened in 1893.

A Competitor in the Wings

"President Elliot recommended to the Trustees of Harvard at the last Commencement, the establishment of a Commercial school. It is on the lines of the Tuck School," Benjamin Kimball wrote to Edward Tuck in July 1907. Kimball added, with evident confidence, "We have the start, and a good one. Our men are doing well and making their mark in the world of business." Indeed, said Kimball, "I was pleased to find matters at Dartmouth in such good running order, and the interest that is being kept up in all departments. Dartmouth men are wanted far and near."

Kimball mirrored the feelings generally held around the campus and its outside constituencies that the college was indeed in good shape. The "New Dartmouth" of President Tucker was no idle piece of braggadocio. Still, the possible appearance of a competitor graduate business school at a university as prestigious as Harvard was not just a peripheral happenstance. Kimball wrote later that year: "I have seen letters from leading concerns in New York to the Dean of the College, inquiring for Tuck students, when they would be available, as they wished more than one, which indicates that they are sought for. One letter said 'A Tuck student comes up to the front quicker than from any other College department,' meaning for practical business. They like them." Not only was the Tuck School faring well, "the College is roving along nicely. We are over-run with students and cannot take them. Had to turn away a hundred. After looking it all over, one more new dormitory of 75 students will be the last dormitory Dartmouth will build, if I have anything to say about it. We are up to the maximum, I think. We can sustain ourselves in great shape with our present number, 1200, and that is large enough for our locality. The country is endorsing Dartmouth to its fullest extent."

Harvard opened its Graduate School of Business Administration in 1908, and its first catalog was impressive. President Tucker wrote Harlow Person, secretary of the Tuck School, in the spring of 1909: "It may interest you to know that Professor C. F. Richardson recently met Mr. Orcutt of the University Press, Cambridge, himself a Harvard man, who told him that he had made a careful study of the catalogues, both of Harvard and of Dartmouth, and that he was confident that the Tuck School program was in advance of the program of the new school of finance at Harvard, that if he were to go to any school he should take the Tuck School." Despite the confidence being expressed by both Kendall and Tucker, there *was* an element of bravado about it all. Clearly, a strong new business school shepherded by formidable Harvard and located just over the border in Massachusetts, the state so important to Dartmouth in terms of enrollment, was likely to be a challenge.

The enrollment at Tuck continued to grow, with seven graduates in 1906–7, nine the next year, and ten in the academic year 1908–9. The Tuck School announcement for 1906–7 included a list of all of the graduates, with their separate employment for the first five years of the school's short life. The positions were impressive—of the total of twenty-four, a number of the graduates held posts that were patently middle management. In spite of the school's modest offerings in the marketing fields, some ten or so of the jobs were definitely marketing posts, and several others could well have been (exact assignments not being given for some of the men). There were at least four bankers, and several graduates had gone into insurance compa- nies. One of the twenty-four was listed in the railroad industry, as general bookkeeper to the general auditor of the Rock Island Rail- road in Chicago; this must have pleased Edward Tuck. James F. Drake had had several positions (or perhaps held all these positions at once): he was secretary of the Springfield, Massachusetts, Board of Trade; vice president of that agency; secretary and treasurer and head of the commercial department of the Home Correspondence School; treasurer of the Morse Motor Vehicle Company; and secre- tary of the Connecticut River Navigation Company. Henry N. Teague was assistant steward at the Hotel Gotham in New York City. Two of the men were stationed overseas with their companies: Victor M. Cutter was a division superintendent for the United Fruit Com- pany in Costa Rica, and Wilfred D. Whittemore was a subaccoun- tant with the International Banking Corporation in Shanghai, China. Several others were involved in foreign trade operations—Raymond

Victor Cutter, Tuck class of 1904, on an early assignment in Central America for United Fruit Company. Courtesy Dartmouth College Library.

The "triennial anniversary" of the Dartmouth class of 1902, held in 1905;
Tuck's James F. Drake holds "Tattledo's" leash. Courtesy Dartmouth College Library.

E. Paine, for example, was the buyer on the west coast of South
America for the American Trading Company. One student, William
R. Gray, had joined the Tuck School as an instructor in accounting
and mathematics (he had taken his MCS at Tuck in 1905 and later
went on to become dean of the school).

There was a wide range in the total-career success stories of the
twenty-four men. Several rose to senior general management positions. Two were chief executive officers for major national corporations: James F. Drake (called Colonel Drake from his service in
World War I) headed Gulf Oil Company for more than two decades,
and Victor Cutter stayed with United Fruit Company to become its
president in 1924, also briefly headed Revere Sugar Company, then
in 1934 became chairman of the New England Planning Commission
as a regional chairman of the National Resources Planning Board.
Percy O. Dorr founded and headed an investment firm carrying his
name in Springfield, Massachusetts. Richard Ward first became

president of a fabric company in Lawrence, Massachusetts, then a bank president. Wilfred Whittemore stayed in international banking, holding posts in China, Japan, and the Philippines until returning to a bank vice presidency in Darien, Connecticut. Henry N. Teague (Colonel Teague) had a long career in hotel management, most often as lessee and manager, then brought back to life the moribund Mt. Washington Railroad as a tourist attraction in New Hampshire. William Gray stayed with Tuck School for his entire career; in 1922 he was elected national president of the fledgling American Association of Collegiate Schools of Business.

Other job assignments among the twenty-four were more middle-management—trust officer, purchasing agent, assistant actuary, manager of a bond department, manufacturers representative, assistant manager of an insurance company, head of the cup division in a paper company, repair manager in a shoe machinery company. Ralph H. Carleton was the railroad person in the group; he stayed in the industry to become assistant general auditor. Many of the graduates had substantial additional international experience, several, for example, living in Argentina for part of their career. But there were others who stayed in one place for their work life; one obituary stated that of all the members of the class, this Tuck graduate "was perhaps the quietest and least voluable . . . his life appears to have been placid and devoid of incident, as his undergraduate career had been."

How Much Independence for Tuck School?

Despite the manifest success of the Tuck graduates to this point, there remained some divisive issues about the extent to which the school was free to run its own operations, and how independent it was from Dartmouth College itself. There were several dimensions of this issue.

First was the quality of its faculty. Some Dartmouth College professors had expressed at the beginning some skepticism about the

quality of the Tuck faculty, just as they had done earlier in relation to the Chandler School faculty (this was the college's less rigorous technical school). Edward Tuck, too, had expressed misgivings from time to time about the same issue. Benjamin Kimball wrote a Wall Street alumnus in May 1910, about this: "I discussed very thoroughly with Mr. Tuck . . . the importance of improving the standard of professorship. . . . He is now and has been very strong in his opinion that the personnel [*sic*] of many of its professors is not up to the standard we wish Dartmouth to attain." It was a matter of money, Tuck felt, and the college was going to need "a large fund" to bring Dartmouth to the standard he desired. As he put it to Bigelow in January 1911, "The pay of full professors has been only $2,600 per annum, on which it is of course impossible to retain for long first-class men." A few of the strongest among the full professors were above this figure; Dixon's salary at this date was $3,600, all but $400 paid by the college and the remainder by Tuck School. But just as Edward Tuck feared, Dixon later left for a faculty post at Princeton. Harlow Person, his successor, developed into a strong leader, widely respected among both the Tuck and the college faculties.

There were other sensitive issues about the faculty. The choice of Tuck's first director, Frank Dixon, the independent and articulate economics professor, had raised concerns at that time about taking such a high-standing person partially away from the Department of Economics. In 1908 new tensions arose over the relationship between the department and Tuck School. A new faculty member had been hired for Tuck, and he just did not seem to be working out. Person wrote Dixon: "The students are practically in revolt against Professor Persons [Warren M. *Persons*, not to be confused with Harlow Person, the secretary of the school], and, so far as I can judge of the situation, it is but little short of a formal protest against his retention as a teacher. The form that it has actually taken is that of a cautious but sullen complaint among themselves, of a terrible cutting of courses in the choosing of electives, of protest . . . on the part of Tuck students who have been required to elect Economics 14, and of the growing opinion among undergraduates that the Tuck School will hardly be worth their while so long as he is on its staff." Persons had been asked to teach several courses in Tuck that had been taught in the Department of Economics, and the students had responded by wanting to avoid the courses. "They are very bitter in their feelings toward Professor Persons (as a teacher, not as a man). They feel the time spent in work under him is wasted; the importance of this lies in the fact that undergraduates accepted this. They say his lectures are 'drool'; that whether he knows the subject or not he teaches nothing."

Secretary Person wrote President Tucker a week later: "Professor Dixon's fears, expressed at the time Professor Persons was being considered, that the Department of Economics was being sacrificed in the interest of the Tuck School, seemed to have been warranted. The Department . . . *has* been sacrificed. On the other hand, the Tuck School has not gained by the sacrifice, for the work in Practical Banking has not been a success, and the work in Statistics and Foreign Exchange only moderately so."

The issue related to the unpopular professor finally was alleviated

"Coming from Tuck School," December 1908: *left to right,* Ernest
Goodrich, Harold Hall, Ed Ford, Inge Fearing, Ralza Cummings.
Courtesy Dartmouth College Library.

by assigning him other courses and moving other professors into his
previous assignments. But this brouhaha had succeeded once more
in bringing to the fore the college's unease about the quality of at
least some of the Tuck faculty. Person came to feel that solving the
organizational position of Tuck would go far toward clearing up am-
biguities about who was responsible for what and which faculty
should teach what course. He prepared a memorandum in April
1909, asking that the president "explain in detail the status of the
School in its relation to the College, and the status of the Director of
the School in his relation to the administration of the School." Person allowed that the status of the director "is one of considerable delicacy." He felt that, in a professional school, centralization of authority and administration in the hands of the director was wisest. He
called attention to the presence of that policy in the Thayer School
and the success of the same policy in the Yale Scientific School. "The
director should not be a clerk of the faculty."

Person elaborated a series of proposed new committees, the sum of which put most of the administrative authority in the hands of the Tuck School itself. A statement was to be constructed that would cover the control of the school over its students, its building, its library, and other equipment. The director would be kept fully informed of the funds being allocated to Tuck; indeed, Person really wanted to segregate funds for Tuck from the remaining massive largesse of Edward Tuck.

Dixon analyzed Person's arguments and, although concurring on many of Person's points, wanted it "to be kept in mind what are legitimate courses of an economics department as determined by the experience of various institutions." He stressed that "no course should be monopolized for Tuck School purposes which can properly be considered to be part of a general economics course." He mentioned specifically the "monopolization of courses in statistics and international trade. . . . My objection is not to the inclusion of this in a Tuck School curriculum but at the monopolization of it."

Sometime before Tucker had received the memorandum and letters from several of the faculty members about it, he had written Dixon on the question of the relationship of the first-year Tuck men to the college. Tucker wanted to make the issue very clear and suggested "the possibility of dividing the first year men into groups according to their outlook for the second year, making all the courses of an academic nature, which it is necessary to put into the Tuck School course, required in common, but giving the men the choice between those technical courses which they wish to carry over into the second year." On the issue of the relationship to the Economics Department, Tucker began, "I hardly see how we can make much progress working at arms end. . . . While it is clear that the Tuck School is founded upon the Department of Economics, the department is at once greater and smaller than the School. How to take out that part of the department which is vital to the School, and give it so distinctive a character that it will count in the sentiment of instructors and students for the School without disturbing the proportions of a department, is a question of so much delicacy that I await your reply before further correspondence." Tucker did allow that he felt that "the faculty of the Tuck School should be made up of men whose work lies almost entirely within that School."

After Person's memorandum had been discussed and refined, it was presented to the board of trustees of the college in April 1909. The trustees formed a two-man subcommittee to confer with Person "with reference to the appointing of an examining or advisory committee on the faculty of that school." President Tucker wrote Person a few days later, "I have not brought the question of the assignment of a distinct part of the Tuck Fund to the Tuck School before the Board for I am not quite sure of the effect. The Tuck School is an evolution, not a ready made affair. It may be as much against as for the School to have a distinct sum set apart. On the whole, I think it will have a better fortune in this regard to work out its own results by gradually defining its capacity than by having its future predetermined by its fund." As to the "examining or advisory committee," Tucker was conciliatory: "There is no haste about the matter unless you wish to have the plan go into effect another year."

Thus, the issue of the college examining committee was left up in the air, particularly so because of an additional factor that had been building over several years and now came to a head.

A "Crippled Leadership"— President Tucker Resigns

Back in May 1905, Edward Tuck received a nine-page handwritten letter from President Tucker. Its contents were startling and upsetting to Tuck. Tucker began with no preliminaries: "I shall be 65 years old the 13th of July. I have been thinking very seriously and talking a good deal with Mrs. Tucker about the fit time for resigning the presidency of the College." He had not mentioned this to anyone else; "I want to write to you, who has been so fine and generous a friend to me and to the College. I want to tell you just how the whole matter looks to me, and to ask you to see if you see any flaw in my judgment."

Tucker began by reciting the need for new buildings over the next two or three years, the jump in enrollment to what was going to be over a thousand, the needs of the library, and the possibilities of a new gymnasium. Further, there were the critical shortfalls in higher salaries for college personnel, particularly the professors. All of these would cumulate to be a figure of something over half a million dollars. Tucker just did not "feel able" to take on the task: "I do not want to play the coward. I remember that Eleazar Wheelock was over 60 years old when he set foot in this wilderness. But I have come to believe in all sincerity that another younger man can do the necessary thing for the College as I cannot." He could see himself as staying with the college in the capacity of a lecturer but nothing much beyond that. No mention of his health was in the Tucker letter.

Tuck responded immediately, suspecting it *was* a problem of health: "You did not tell me of any specific causes of discouragement which have come upon you, but I cannot help feeling that something of the sort has occurred or you would not think of doing what you now suggest." Tuck felt that Tucker had been working too hard and that he perhaps had become overwhelmed by his problems. Still, he did not want to see Tucker resign: "I am free to say that if you cannot do it nobody else can. Dartmouth College without Tucker would be like the play of Hamlet with Hamlet left out. . . . If you should give up the job in the early future, it would be assumed that you found your labour had been in a measure wasted and that something was wrong with the institution which had led you to think the game was not worth the candle." Tuck concluded with a strong caveat: "Dartmouth College reawakened and modernised will be for you the enduring monument of your life if you stick to it and carry on, at least for a few years longer, the work which you have so brilliantly begun." Tucker should schedule longer vacations, "rather than incur the risk of your having to abandon it completely."

Later in the summer, Tucker answered the letter, reciting again the complex financial demands on the college. He continued: "My difficulty then comes in at this point and it is one of a good deal of delicacy. The Trustees are beginning to feel that insofar as I am a personal factor in the growth of the College, its growth is a precarious source of financial support." Tucker explained that he just did not have the strength to do both the inside and the outside work. He wanted to develop and utilize the college's "natural constituencies," and continued: "The only disappointment I have felt has been that your splendid example has not been followed by your contemporaries."

Tuck already had made the decision and now announced that he was giving an endowment for teaching, specifically for the economic well-being of the professors at the end of their careers, what he called "a retiring fund." Tucker was highly enthusiastic. "The Carnegie Fund seems like a charity," Tucker wrote, "largely on account of the ways in which application must be made for it. It is not taking care of our own. I should feel, if you look at things as I do, that the gift [the retiring fund] would crown the noble endowment which stands in your name." Later, in 1907, Tuck furnished additional funds, which would provide for a special retirement fund for Tucker, the sum of $3,000 to be paid to him annually. In 1910, Tuck made a major grant of two thousand shares of Great Northern preferred stock and two thousand shares of Northern Pacific stock, specifically for the improvement of the existing scale of salaries of the faculty throughout the college. Later in that year, Tucker presented a major proposal to the trustees concerning the new building projects. The trustees gave assent to the whole set of proposals, and Tucker seemed relieved and expressed willingness to Tuck to continue on the job.

But all was not well with Tucker's health. In April 1907 he had a heart attack while on an alumni trip, followed by a similar but less acute attack when he returned from the trip. Within a month it was clear that Tucker had to step down, at least from his full, complex duties. There was a brief upset when the news of the impending change became known prematurely. But the facts spoke for themselves. Tucker was pressed by his doctors to resign, and he did so.

It was not an easy position to fill, and Tucker stayed on through the following academic year, 1908–9, even giving the convocation address to welcome the largest-ever Dartmouth enrollment, 1,136 men. Tucker had feared a "crippled leadership," but with the help of acting president John K. Lord and Ernest Martin Hopkins, the secretary of the college, the year passed without further effects on President Tucker's health or any particularly serious college problems. The issue of the Tuck School organization, brought to him in the spring of 1909, was one of the last with which he had dealt. Shortly before commencement, the long-awaited announcement came that a new president had been elected. He was Ernest Fox Nichols, at that time professor of physics at Columbia University and earlier a teacher for five years in the Physics Department of Dartmouth. Nichols was inaugurated as president of Dartmouth in October 1909. Tucker spoke that day and welcomed Nichols to the "Wheelock Succession."

"The New Reservation of Time"

" This is an example of a good book hidden under the bushel of a bad title. No one would know without reading a part of the book what the 'new reservation of time' meant, and the term would not arouse the most curious book-buyer" (*Baltimore Sun*). But the newspaper was wrong: the book by William Jewett Tucker published under that name and his earlier article on the same subject in the *Atlantic Monthly* received wide acclaim. The article came out just a few months after Tucker retired in June 1909. Tucker was grappling with the implications of his retirement. In his autobiography, *My Generation,* he called his previous two years in office, after he learned of his heart condition, "two years of crippled leadership." How should one cope with ". . . that unhoped serene That men call age" (his quotation from an unnamed source). In his introspective *Atlantic* article, he described the "new principle" of providing retirement benefits, such as Edward Tuck and Dartmouth College had tendered to him. The earlier years were for "associated" labor, and the new benefits provisions fixed retirement at between sixty and seventy years (Tucker was at

been if certain great men that we have known or read about could have appreciated the wisdom of that statement that I never before have seen in print." By the time the book was published, Tuck, too, was over seventy.

Tuck continued, "I sympathize with you fully in all that you say regarding 'The New Reservation of Time.' We will all put up the best fight we can against Anno Domini but sooner or later we must yield. I hope the comfort and rest you are getting in your own library will prolong your life and enjoyment yet for many years. Those who have to take care of themselves very often outlive those who do not." (Certainly, Tuck was one who took care of himself and his wife very well.)

In the first decade of his retirement, Tucker wrote widely, with thoughtful and relevant pieces that addressed many issues of the day. *The Atlantic* was his favorite venue, and there he wrote on the "goal of equality," on the social conscience, and when the war came, on its ethical challenge and on the peace process he envisioned. A number of other articles also came out during this first decade of his retirement, culminating in his comprehensive and very evocative autobiography, *My Generation* (1919). He participated only modestly in college events; Leon Richardson, perhaps the most analytical of all the Dartmouth College historians over the years, wrote: "Of necessity, he came to be a recluse in the Hanover of which he had been the central figure so long, and to those who had lived in the College in the days of his leadership, it appealed with a deep sense of pathos that his career had passed into the traditions of the College, that successive generations of undergraduates came to regard him as a great figure of the past, very much as they looked upon the founder of the College, while, in actual fact, he was still alive in their midst." He died in September 1926, at the age of eighty-seven.

Tucker left a powerful legacy, one that ranked along with that of the Reverend Eleazar Wheelock, the founder of the college. Tucker's powers of analysis and his clarity in laying out the fundamental nature of the problems at hand were legendary. The most frequent response by others on hearing a Tucker exposition was to turn immediately to possible solutions, accepting fully Tucker's clear and simple statements of often very complex problems. His personality was such that, as Richardson put it, he "was endowed with the qualities which won to him the attention of other men even upon a casual meeting, which quickly aroused their admiration upon further acquaintance and which brought to him their sincere love when they came really to know him well. To few men in position can have come so many manifestations of high devotion." Tucker had dignity without pompousness, a tact that was combined with a play of humor. Yet he also was an effective disciplinarian. The students came to a quick understanding of his candor and openness of mind, yet his decisiveness when the question came to the point was legendary. Tucker was not at all fond of overly involved or esoteric scholarship, although he certainly respected academic competence and vigorously defended academic freedom, even when opposition was strong (as he had done in his response to Edward Tuck's brief challenge of and attack on faculty independence). Richardson concluded, "A single word sums up the salient characteristics of the President and that word is wisdom."

But as Richardson pointed out, all of these qualities were not yet the essence of the man, for the students saw him as speaking from the center of the life of the individual. Tucker was a minister, and religion permeated his involvement in the college. He was not heavy-handed in this, and the students flocked to his Sunday vespers, even if they themselves were not religiously inclined.

Richardson frankly pointed out that Tucker was not as much of an educational force as some of his colleagues in other Ivy League institutions: "As an educational pioneer, Dr. Tucker was not preeminent. No novel educational policy was entered upon during his administration, unless, perhaps, the establishment of the Tuck School is to be placed in that category." Richardson attributed most of this to Tucker's lack of resources during his tenure: "Considering the slender means at the disposal of the institution, it was a work of great magnitude merely to raise it to a plane of equality with the best foundations of the land. . . . It was not a time at Dartmouth for radical educational experimentation." It is interesting that Richardson, writing his definitive book on the college, mentioned the Tuck School as a potential true innovation. We now have the perspective of sixty-five-plus years of additional experience since he wrote this, with the

amazing growth of graduate business schools around the country and
with the tremendous strength of the schools on the leading edge of
that growth. In the founding of the Tuck School as the first example
of this important American institution, the judgment of Richardson
seems quite prophetic.

A Shoulder to the Wheel, Once Again

During the two-year search period for a new Dartmouth president, Edward Tuck had himself made a recommendation: Arthur Sherburne Hardy, who had been professor of mathematics at
the college and later United States ambassador to Spain. Benjamin
Kimball knew this individual and at once corroborated Tuck's opinion that he was an accomplished and able man, "well fitted for taking
the Presidency of the College in case of need." As Tuck knew him
only slightly, the recommendation was not pushed too hard, although
Tuck did write Kimball: "His selection as successor to Dr. Tucker (if
he is the man I judge him to be) would greatly stimulate my interest
in the old institution." In the spring of 1909, Dr. Nichols, instead of
Hardy, had been chosen as Tucker's successor.

Tuck had met Nichols on an earlier visit and seemed genuinely
pleased at the choice. Early in 1911, Tuck shared his private feelings
about his benefactions at Dartmouth with his friend John Bigelow,
who had written to praise him for them:

> The institution has a glorious past . . . with a prestige which it would be
> wicked to allow to be destroyed by the poverty of its financial re-
> sources. Dr. Nichols, the new President, is a very strong man, possess-
> ing all the ability, educational and administrative, requisite to the suc-
> cessful management of an institution of learning. But the res angustae
> domi [the limited resources of the institution] is heavily felt by the Col-
> lege even in the economical surroundings of northern New Hamp-
> shire. . . . With the boost I have given, all hands are very cheerful and

A distinguished Franco-American entente: *left to right,* General John J. Pershing, General Henri J. E. Gouraud, U.S. Ambassador to France Walter E. Edge, Edward Tuck, and *at far right,* U.S. Secretary of State Henry L. Stimson. Courtesy Dartmouth College Library.

enthusiastic, and I believe New Hampshire's most famous institution will now be able to hold its head up along side even the wealthier but newer ones of the West, as one of the first colleges on the land.

Still, Tuck had become increasingly concerned about the quality of the Dartmouth College faculty, and let his views be known strongly to Tucker and to others. Tucker had written to him of two large estates that had come to the college shortly after Tucker stepped down, and Tuck replied with some of his advice: "The Hitchcock estate is certainly a most valuable asset to the College and comes to it in a good time. To develop it to the greatest advantage will require careful consideration and a good deal of money, but fortunately there is no need of haste. The essential thing is to make no mistakes in the general plan. The scheme can be worked out from year to year as the necessary money is found. I judge from what Mr. Kimball has written me that considerable work is being laid out for the current year to take care of the present growth of the College." Tuck then added a blunt comment that characterized his views about student and faculty quality: "I am glad to see that there is a considerable weeding out of the unfittest at the periodic student examinations."

Apparently, Tuck had been mulling over in his own mind whether another of his gifts should be made at this point, once again to give impetus to a new administration and to push to get alumni to contribute more. In November 1910 he made the decision mentioned earlier, to give the two thousand shares of Great Northern preferred stock and two thousand shares of Northern Pacific stock for "improvement of the existing scale of salaries of the faculty of the College in all of its departments." The gift represented, in 1910 dollars, a value of $500,000. This very large gift was all the more remarkable for the fact that Tuck was not in as good a financial position as in earlier years. As he mentioned to John Bigelow, in the letter quoted in the previous paragraph, "It was not quite convenient for me just at this time to do what I did, but I felt that the moment was very critical for the College and that to give now would be the equivalent to giving double the amount ten years hence." He wrote Tucker a few days later, "I have felt that the institution needed money very much and very soon if the brilliant opening of Dr. Nichols' career was to be maintained and the onward progress of the College inaugurated by you was to be carried along still further." He drew once again on the same imagery he had used with Bigelow: "It would have been wicked to allow the old College to starve to death."

James J. Hill: A Revelation

The tenuous situation of the railroads caused a considerable part of Edward Tuck's financial tensions. "[They] have been hounded enough," he wrote Tucker at the time he made the gift. "The one cheap commodity in America today is railroad transportation—it costs one-half or two-thirds what it does in Europe, with a much

James J. Hill, Glacier Park, Montana, 1913. Photo © 1987, 1998 The James J. Hill Group, St. Paul, Minnesota.

better service. There is no oppression of the people, with passenger rates at $.02 a mile and freight rates cheaper still in proportion. Of course, it is always popular to attack the corporations, the innocent as well as the guilty. But if agitation against the railroads continues much longer, then Dartmouth College had better sell out its Great Northern and Northern Pacific stocks while it still can get par or above for them." He would have considered this an absolute apostasy if someone had said that to him in 1900!

Tuck had kept up his correspondence with James J. Hill, his letters filled with queries for information from the canny, uncommunicative railroad baron. Tuck's campaign for many years to persuade Hill to visit Hanover and Dartmouth College had misfired every time. Hill was just "too busy," always off on some new venture of which only he himself knew the details. Tucker signaled that he, for one, had become chary of asking: "I hesitate to broach the subject to him again, in any form, unless I can be pretty sure it would be agreeable to him."

Hill, too, was feeling the pangs of age; he was one year older than William Jewett Tucker, three years older than Tuck. In 1912, Hill gave up the chairmanship of the Great Northern, passing the mantle to his son Louis. During this period, he was putting into order his own financial affairs, affairs that only he himself fully knew.

In 1914, Hill made an exception to his oft-expressed caveat that he never wanted a building or professorship named after him. One of the senior partners of J. P. Morgan's firm, Thomas W. Lamont, had established at the Harvard Graduate School of Business Administration the "James J. Hill Professorship of Railroad Transportation," complete with $125,000 in pledges for its funding. Hill was delighted, consented to the use of his name, and, finding that an additional $125,000 was still needed, contributed that entire sum himself. He insisted that the recipient not be just a theorist and that the chosen professor spend several months on the Hill railroads learning about "Western railroading." None of Tuck's letters to Hill during this period mentions this, but it must have been a sore disappointment to him that the gift did not go to Dartmouth for the Tuck School.

In 1915, President Nichols decided once again to attempt to interest James J. Hill in the college, specifically by offering Dartmouth's honorary degree one more time. This time Hill surprised everyone by accepting, replying to Nichols, "D.V. [Deo volente, "God willing"] I expect to be with you on June 18th [1916]."

But this was not to be. On May 27, 1916, just three weeks before the long-awaited Dartmouth visit, Hill died, after having been in a coma for several weeks. There appears to be no record of whether Edward Tuck went to the funeral. It would have been a long trip, and Tuck's reluctance to leave France for any reason would probably have been in play here.

There is an enigmatic reference in the Beckles Willson papers that described Hill's efforts to put together a huge mortgage covering the Great Northern that would authorize some $600 million worth of bonds. Willson had become a good friend of the Tucks, living near them in Paris, and had begun to work on a biography of Edward Tuck (never completed) which he planned to call "A New-Englander in France: The Life of Edward Tuck, Citizen of Paris." What was not revealed at that time, according to Willson, was that Hill was secretly unloading part of his own holdings of stock in the company while continuing to press his closest friends who were stockholders (Tuck still, of course, being one) to hold onto their interests unimpaired (in order not to depress the price). In March 1914, George Baker wrote Tuck, "About the ore property, I don't know what to say to you and feel pretty well disgusted to be kept in such ignorance about it. Hill doesn't volunteer anything and *I won't ask him*. Fond as I am of him, it is a great disappointment."

When Hill died, Great Northern stock had fallen, and even the ore properties were not returning dividends. Tuck wrote Kimball in 1918: " The investment in Ore Certificates . . . has been to me a source of great disappointment. . . . The returns on them have been far less than Mr. James J. Hill had anticipated and so confidently predicted to us they would be. It is to restore and make good to the Endowment Fund the unexpected depreciation . . . that I now add this amount of shares to those previously held" (he increased the college's holding of 1,230 shares by an additional 2,770 from his own portfolio). In 1926, expressing that he was "greatly disappointed and mortified" with the ore certificates that had been owned by the college, he traded them back to himself for "security credible" (his words) new stocks, giving the college shares of Chase Bank, Tidewater Oil, and Continental Insurance. By 1930 he was concerned also about the college's Great Northern and Northern Pacific stock holdings (gifts from him): "I am considerably worried over the College's large holdings. . . . I had never foreseen or even thought of the destructive competition of motor trucks with railroad traffic." The effects of the Great Depression drove both stocks further down, and in 1933, Tuck lamented to Hopkins, "I am mortified that the College should be such a sufferer from my excess of faith in James J. Hill."

Several years later, according to Willson, Tuck wrote his nephew: "The end of Hill's life was a complete failure. His wild dreams have proved to be perfect delusion. He captured me early and I am sorry to say my life over here prevented me from discovering what some others did discover, that his judgment and advice had become bad. To find, too, after his death, that he had sold out nearly all his holdings, both railroad and ore properties, without notice to his friends, whom he had urged so constantly and forcibly to invest in and hold, was the worst business shock I have ever experienced. However, I am still alive and solvent, though my fortune has diminished very heavily."

When the biography of Hill was to be published, his son Louis sent a copy to Tuck. Beckles Willson told the story this way in his papers: "Tuck smiled indulgently about the luminous panegyric which concealed all its hero's faults and exaggerated his achievements. 'Jim Hill' he said, 'was undeniably able, but he was the most selfish man I have ever known. Everyone in his orbit must be tributary to him. Whoever else was deprived in whatever sacrifices had to be made, he took pains to ensure that not a single dollar should be forthcoming from his own pocket.'"

The documentation for this story of Hill's alleged disloyalty to his friends is no longer extant. But we know that Tuck had been worried about just this kind of eventuality and even had been called to task by George F. Baker in 1908 for telling his nephew about hearing rumors of private selling of blocs of Great Northern stock. Tuck wrote directly to Hill at that time, "Have not some large holders of Great Northern been selling their stock? . . . If so, you who have access to the stock list must know who it is." Hill did not respond. The story related by Willson that Hill himself had sold without telling his friends would have taken place several years later. If it did happen, it did not bankrupt Tuck, for he made major gifts to Dartmouth College and elsewhere after this time.

A New Tuck School

In 1913, Tuck made a gift to the college of five hundred shares of preferred stock of the Great Northern to promote among the students of the college a more intimate knowledge of the French language and of French thought and civilization. "My desire," Tuck wrote, "is that our graduates in so far as it may be given them to influence public opinion concerning the French nation may, from their fuller understanding and appreciation of French culture and ideals, assist to bring about an ever closer friendship between two peoples

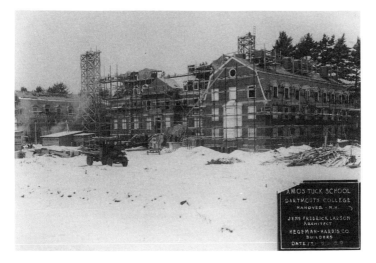

A new Tuck School under construction, December 1929. Courtesy Dartmouth
College Library.

already united by many bonds of sympathy and of historic association, and separated only by difference of speech." Some part of this
was to be used for the employment of a professor of the French language, and additional amounts were allocated to defray the expenses
of conferences and lectures. There were several further large gifts to
the Amos Tuck endowment fund to augment its total.

In 1922, Tuck asked that the name of the fund be changed to the
Edward Tuck Endowment Fund. He explained this: "I have no special vanity about it, but it seems to me that my own name better be
connected with the Fund so that future generations may not ignore
entirely my connection with it." In that same year he gave additional
shares, in this case of the Electric Storage Battery Co., to provide mo-
nies to build "a new and appropriate residence for the President,
worthy of the College with its high standing and reputation."

In 1928 came another stunning Tuck School gift. The school's
great success by this time had persuaded the trustees that new quarters were necessary. The location was to be on the Hitchcock estate,
on the westerly axis of the president's house and between Tuck Drive

Edward Tuck paid for the restoration of La Turbie,
overlooking the Mediterranean Sea, built in 6 B.C. by
Emperor Augustus. Courtesy Dartmouth College Library.

and an extension of a proposed mall from Baker Library. Tuck told
George Baker, "Hopkins never asked me for the money to do this,
but only my permission to put up and move into a new group of
buildings, which the Tuck School's success made an absolute necessity. I consented, but only on condition that nobody's money but my
own should ever go into the School, which I had founded in memory
of my father and wished to keep."

After an initial appropriation from the Edward Tuck Fund of
$125,000 and credit for a like amount for the old Tuck building, con-
struction began. A year later, six hundred shares of Chase stock were
sold, netting $569,766.50 for the construction. Tuck then wrote, with

his customary aplomb, "I dislike vulgar fractions," and mailed a check for $5,233.50 to bring the total to an even $575,000.

The new Tuck School was a multibuilding complex: a central administration hall, with offices, classrooms, and a library (to be named after Tuck); a high-ceiling refectory reminiscent of an English baronial dining room, to be called Stell Hall after Julia's maiden name; and two dormitories, Salmon P. Chase House and Levi Woodbury House. Salmon Chase was an 1826 Dartmouth graduate and later chief justice of the U.S. Supreme Court; he was presiding officer at the impeachment trial of President Andrew Johnson. Levi Woodbury, class of 1809, was governor of New Hampshire, then U.S. Senator, secretary of both the navy and treasury, and finally, a justice of the U.S. Supreme Court until his death in 1841.

Edward Tuck died in April 1938 at the age of ninety-five. In February 1993 the Edward Tuck Fund's separately invested assets were moved to the college's main endowment at a value then of $36,398,422.33. This is a remarkable figure but still does not fully represent the wide range of Edward and Julia Tuck's benefactions. There were dozens more gifts to Dartmouth, several large donations in Edward's beloved state of New Hampshire, and almost countless beneficent acts, monetary and otherwise, in France. One of the most important was his gift in 1930 of the art in his Champs-Elysées apartment to the Petit Palais in Paris, a first-rank collection that included Boucher tapestries and paintings, Sèvres and Chinese porcelains, eighteenth-century French enameled watches, and (especial Tuck favorites) a Greuze portrait, an Houdon bust, and a Graffieri statuette, all of Benjamin Franklin, so admired by Tuck.

What now can be said of this man Edward Tuck?

Edward Tuck, Citizen

Over the forty-nine years that Edward and Julia Tuck lived in France year-round, the French people came to have the highest regard for them; indeed, to say that there was a mutual love affair between the Tucks and the French would give to it a Francophile patina. Edward, made chevalier in the Legion of Honor in 1906, was promoted successively to officier, commandeur, and grand officier. Then the crowning honor: in 1929 he was awarded the Grand Cross of the Legion of Honor; at that time only ten other Americans had been recognized with this renowned citation.

But the encomium that seems most to epitomize Edward Tuck came three years later, in 1932. On the eve of the July 14 celebrations in Paris and in recognition of his approaching ninetieth birthday, the Paris Municipal Council made him an honorary Citizen of the Republic. Somehow, the concept of "citizen" seems so right, seems to capture a whole gamut of attributes and values characterized by Tuck.

Julia, too, was accorded many honors. She was chevalier and then officier in the Legion of Honor, and was accorded several medals, one (the Prix de Vertu of the Académie Française) with Edward. At a meeting of the Academy of Sciences, the widow of the famous French astronomer, Camille Flammarion, herself also an astronomer, named a new planetoid *Tuckia* after Julia. *Time* magazine, in a major article on Edward in November 1930, said it was because of "his interest in science." But this does not make much sense—Tuck had little such interest. More likely, it was because of regard for Julia.

The attributes of Edward were manifold. He was endowed with high intelligence. Second in his graduating class at Dartmouth and just accorded Phi Beta Kappa, he gave the class oration at that commencement. His address emphasized the liberal arts, and he observed that the "ability to distinguish" was "focused" by these liberating experiences. Tuck was well read and well written: he published several dozen articles in major critical journals, concentrating particularly on monetary policy. He held high standards—for Dartmouth students, for Dartmouth faculty, for himself (witness his acute perception in his collecting of the best in the arts).

He lived a life of true privilege; his wealth and its uses tend to dominate any evaluation of his life. And he was generous, never needing a push or an entreaty, seeming almost to sense a new problem or

Hôpital Stell near Vert-Mont, Military Hospital No. 66 during World War I.
Courtesy Dartmouth College Library.

need. He gave unequivocally and most of the time did not want to intrude in the management of the given effort. This could be stated as "always" in his later years: he grew significantly over his lifetime in walking the sensitive line between showing abiding interest and supportive cheerleading without courting, even subtly, obsequiousness or complaisance. The star-crossed attempt at corralling criticism of the railroads by the faculty (specifically that of the economist Frank Dixon) was the most pronounced case of the latter and was neutralized adroitly by President Tucker. Although Tuck would not publicly temper his feelings at the time, the tenor of his views did seem to mellow more or less immediately afterward. Later, Tuck and Ernest Martin Hopkins, who followed Nichols as president in 1916, became very fond of each other; Hopkins spoke out on many controversial social issues, but Tuck never second-guessed him.

Tuck had little or no sympathy for wealth for its own sake. He continually railed against the selfishness and narrow-mindedness of his own peers in the business and financial communities and of those of

"The Hired Man," photo taken at Bois-Préau, July 1926. Courtesy Dartmouth College Library.

inherited means when they made less than thoughtful use of their wealth. In the little cemetery of St. Germain, near Vert-Mont, where both Edward and Julia are buried, a Benjamin Franklin passage is carved into the Aberdeen granite: "The years roll by and the last will come, when I would rather have it said 'He lived usefully' than 'He died rich.'" Many of the private comments in the trove of personal letters reiterate this strongly held antipathy toward idle wealth. As Horatio Krans, the director of the American University Union in Paris, put it in 1932, "He was . . . a heretic as regards one article, which has . . . slipped into the American creed—the article which exalts being busy, for the sake of being busy or as the road to wealth, to the rank of a cardinal virtue."

The only example in Tuck's papers of outright acquisitiveness occurred when the famous Table des Marechaux, a Sèvres-made piece of furniture ordered by Napoleon himself to commemorate the victory of Solferino, came on the market and Tuck found himself bidding against William Randolph Hearst. Tuck resolved to have it even if it "took away the butter" for his bread, and he did win it, for $16,000. There was no further report on the butter.

Tuck's social skills were reputed to be and must have been legendary. He was a gracious and princely host, could hold his own in any company, from the highest to the most modest, and thoroughly enjoyed people at every level. Friendly, open, and plebian, he equally relished the charged, sophisticated, sometimes brittle conversations in the salon at his and Julia's "82" and his own haying with his modest friends and neighbors in the Vert-Mont fields. Once he had a snapshot made of himself working in those fields, lettered "hired man" at the bottom to "surprise and amuse Julia." He sent a copy to one of his friends and received a prompt reply: "Now, about the Hired Man. The pitchfork and the hay are all right; but when I was a hired man, I didn't have creased trousers or that kind of a straw hat; and, oh, not a stand-up collar and fancy four-in-hand tie. Well, times do change."

The two Tucks had put enormous energy and much money into building and supervising the Hospital Stell in the village next to the estate. It eventually had sixty beds and accomplished a truly yeoman contribution during World War I. The Tucks bought several ambulances, which were quartered in the garages of Vert-Mont and used to bring wounded Allied soldiers to Hospital Stell. Edward also acquired a nearby farm just to provision the hospital during the war. Earlier, Julia also founded a School of Domestic Economy in the village, to train young girls in homemaking.

The intimacy of having so many articulate and revealing letters, both from and to Tuck, has allowed a deeper view of Tuck's values, aspirations, many hopes, some fears, and even just what tickled his fancy. His intense friendship with John Bigelow, as seen in their many letters, particularly begins to sketch the whole person, for both men. Here one sees their preoccupation with politics; this particular time, at the turn of the century and shortly thereafter, was an amazingly evocative and rich period for the country, and the papers mirrored many of these tensions, as well as the opportunities. Edward saw—and lived—all of this.

Leon Richardson, in his *History of Dartmouth College*, ends his section on William Jewett Tucker: "A single word sums up the salient characteristics of the president and that word is wisdom." Conceivably, this could be said for Edward Tuck, too. I will say it somewhat differently and will use two words: in the best and broadest sense, Edward Tuck was an *exemplary citizen*.

One Hundred Years

It was easy to define the success of the Tuck School over its first two decades by most conventional measures. The marketplace, of course, was crucial. Had the Tuck School done the job? Were its graduates better young businessmen—were they preferentially accepted by businesses, and were they moving up the ladder to higher-level specialist or, better still, general management responsibilities? Did Dartmouth College gain in that mystical, ill-defined hierarchy of complex values by which all colleges and universities are measured and that rate a very few "best," a larger number as "excellent," and the rest as "good" or in some purgatory below? The answer to all these questions seems to be emphatically yes. The almost instantaneous and widespread positive responses testified to the need articulated first by Tucker, confirmed by Tuck, adopted as a mantra in the successive announcements, and believed by most (but, given ever-present interdepartmental rivalries, not all) of the faculty and administration. Tuck School was a good fit for "the New Dartmouth" of Tucker. Little or nothing that happened in its first quarter-century detracted from this initial judgment—nor in the next three, but that is beyond the time period encompassed in this story.

The context of the times, especially the last decade of the nineteenth and the first of the twentieth centuries, while bringing enormous challenges for business, gave the business schools an auspicious opportunity. The pace of business had become faster, galvanized by wide swings in political leadership and an onrush of technological and managerial innovations—indeed, revolutions. The scientific management movement burgeoned, new forms of organization

The Tuck School machine room in World War II, c. May 1945. Courtesy
Dartmouth College Library.

structure evolved. Alfred D. Chandler Jr., in his path-breaking book
that won both Pulitzer and Bancroft prizes, *The Visible Hand: The
Managerial Revolution in American Business*, wrote: "As the twentieth
century opened, the new integrated multifunctional, often multina-
tional enterprise was becoming the most influential institution in the
American economy. . . . Central to the professionalization of management were modern business schools [and] in the decade after 1899,
business education became part of the curriculum of the nation's
most prestigious colleges and universities."

Tuck School became an exciting place for faculty. There was a
sense of movement and new directions both in preparing graduates
for business and in constructing the pedagogical underpinnings for
this specialist education. This was a fresh endeavor, not yet claiming
to be a formal discipline, let alone a profession that could join the traditional three: law, medicine, and theology. The clash was nowhere
better seen at Dartmouth than in the relationship of the Department
of Economics to Tuck School. There was a several-hundred-year history for formal economics, with its distinguished forebears like David
Ricardo, Thomas Malthus, Adam Smith, and others. The interface to
the Tuck curriculum and courses was not an easy one to manage.

The 3/2 academic mode, with its first three years undergraduate work, a fourth year of business basics as a combined senior year and first graduate year, and a second year of full graduate studies, added complications. It was advantageous in the sense that it allowed both undergraduate liberal arts and graduate training in five years. In the fourth year this inevitably brought a mix of two cultures and two significantly different pedagogical climates, not to mention the shift from an undergraduate social milieu to a graduate one. In melding the two, did this program starve either? For the undergraduate finishing his liberal arts, probably not much, if careful course selections were made. On the graduate side, perhaps there was more of a compromise if traditional undergraduate senior-level courses were taught solely as such. President Tucker grappled with this and at one point (noted earlier) proposed and later discarded the idea of setting up a two-culture separation between those leaving after the fourth year and those wanting to complete the MCS degree.

The 3/2 program had some other drawbacks that, at the same time, turned out to be advantages. The candidates for the Tuck program were mostly selected straight from the undergraduate body at the college; there were provisions made to accept men from the outside, but this was infrequent. So the Tuck student body particularly tended toward homogeneity, with the associated impediment that it introduced no fresh blood with different experiences. There were, however, the advantages of a continuation of the fabled Dartmouth loyalty, comradeship, and "corporate consciousness," to use Tucker's words in his inaugural speech. Edward Tuck's foresight in giving the original Tuck School building (now McNutt), which with its spacious and thoughtful inside layout became available and open by 1904, was fortuitous, enhancing this "Dartmouth bonding" almost from the start. To the present, this ambiance has remained as a signal competitive plus.

Harvard's Graduate School of Business Administration opened its first year in October 1908, with thirty-three full-time students. All had four-year college degrees, most from Harvard College. In this regard, it *was* different from Tuck in requiring the baccalaureate, and in 1924 this led to an embarrassing contretemps for Harvard. Edward

Tuck's good friend George Baker had been approached by William Lawrence, an Episcopal bishop, member of the Harvard Corporation, and chairman of its development subcommittee, who was soliciting gifts to Harvard University in a joint effort by the Department of Fine Arts, the Department of Chemistry, and the Business School. Lawrence told of the visit: "Baker said . . . if, by giving five million dollars I could have the privilege of building the whole School, I should like to do it. If it were one of several such schools or an old story, I should not care to do it, but my life has been given to business, and I should like to found the first Graduate School, and give a new start to better business standards. I want to do it alone." Apparently, Baker was assured that Harvard was "the first Graduate School." This claim, if made literally, would fly in the face of mainstream writing on business schools in the United States; the 1959 report of the Carnegie Series in American Education, Frank Pierson's *Education of American Businessmen*, recognizes Tuck as the first graduate business school, and an influential new book, *MBA: The First Century* (1998), opens with a description of the founding of the Tuck School: "Thus it was that . . . seven young men [from the first two years' classes] marched down the aisle in Hanover, New Hampshire and received their MCS . . . diplomas, thereby becoming the first graduate-degreed businessmen in all the world."

After agreeing to the Harvard gift, Baker promptly left for Paris, with plans for a visit with Edward Tuck. It was a meeting of unexpected revelations, as recounted to President Hopkins by Tuck: "Baker told me this was the first Business School ever established by any university in the United States and was having very great success, whereupon I said to him that I had established one at Dartmouth over twenty years ago. This surprised him greatly. He is quite deaf and misunderstood me and said: 'I know it is not the only one, but it is the first one.' Fortunately I had here a copy of your last year's Tuck School bulletin . . . he took it away with him saying he would read it through with much interest. . . . Evidently Baker had been told by the Harvard people that theirs was the first and original Business School and he had given them full credit for it."

Eventually, the Harvard people modified the statement, holding finally that the Harvard Business School was the first graduate school of business that required its entrants to hold a bachelor's degree. Hopkins called the earlier version "not a meticulously accurate statement," blaming some of the older group of Harvard graduates in their "superciliousness and egotistic self-satisfaction." Tuck put this thought even more bluntly in his response to Hopkins: "I never talk of the College with Harvard men, whose conceit and self-complacency allow of no interest in or comparison with a smaller institution."

Baker, once he knew the facts, seemed not to be nonplussed by them. Later, he had a "chuckle" about it (his words) when he met President Hopkins. Baker followed through with his huge gift, and the superb library on the Harvard campus bearing his name was soon in place (the school itself was to be known as the George F. Baker Foundation). Baker also had a Dartmouth graduate in his family, his uncle, Fischer Ames Baker, class of 1859 (just before Edward Tuck matriculated). So Baker sent a smaller gift of $100,000 to Dartmouth for scholarships just after giving the Harvard grant. A few months later Tuck wrote to Baker about the college's need for a new library: "Dartmouth has perhaps the finest college Gymnasium building in the United States . . . it would be a great thing if the same could be said of its Library . . . If you should feel that you could give [the Library], I should be very happy to think that your and my name were associated together, [that] there be a 'Baker Library' as well as a Tuck School." Baker, unable to resist his old friend, succumbed and agreed to tender the million dollars. "I doubt if I would have been so interested," he wrote Tuck, "had it not been for your seductive letter to me." After the crash of 1929, Tuck additionally cajoled Baker into a second million-dollar gift, for the maintenance of Baker Library, pointing out to him, "a million dollars is not what it used to be."

Tuck's increasing emphasis on a central focus on general management throughout the Tuck School curriculum fitted very well with the needs and demands of business. In this, Tuck was the leader and continuing advocate. In Frank Pierson's Carnegie report, he wrote, "Very early in the formation of business schools, attention was paid to the manager or administrator role in business. Usually the management viewpoint came in a single course. . . . At Tuck and some-

what later at Chicago, it was developed rather systematically in a series of courses." (Pierson gave similar credit to Harvard, when it
started such a focus under Wallace Donham in 1919.) Tuck's program
also included "clinic work," involving field experiences with local
businesses and chambers of commerce. Hanover's isolation in those
early years required creative solutions; better roads later and the air-
plane after World War II made the plan more practicable.

It is not just coincidental in viewing today's Amos Tuck School of
Business Administration (its name since 1945) to do so, as I have,
through the eyes of its two founders, those two fast friends, the sedu-
lous, vigorous educator William Jewett Tucker and the courtly, generous philanthropist Edward Tuck. The two saw the world of business
right from the first in its broadest, most encompassing embodiment.
Tucker's letter from London to Professors Colby and Wells, his two
Dartmouth faculty colleagues, on April 26, 1899, asked the question
(in regard to "our graduates who go into business") whether "we can
give them a better training, *commensurate with the larger meaning of
business as it is now understood?*" (my emphasis). Both Tucker and
Tuck centered their perspective on the manager, in a general management context. Both were "global" in their thinking; Tuck, especially, exemplified a two-continent, worldly approach to business (although his particular obsession with the railroads sometimes made
him somewhat more focused on one industry). Tucker perceptively
had recognized the broader context of business—and its insularity,
too—in his inaugural address on becoming Dartmouth's president, a
half dozen years before he and Tuck sat down to their historic discus-
sions in the latter's apartment in Paris.

Now, as the twenty-first century approaches, the very year that
Tuck School celebrates its hundredth year as the country's oldest
graduate business school, business itself (domestic and global) demands broad-gauged, general management–oriented, globally trained
leaders. The marketplace is the ultimate measure of success; businesses vote with their pocketbooks in recruiting graduates from the
various business schools. Those schools positioned by both their past
focus and their present dedication to find and train young men and

Edward Tuck in the salon of the Tucks' Château de
Vert-Mont, near Paris. Courtesy Dartmouth College Library.

women in a general management mode are especially in demand
today. By its past dedication and present performance, Tuck is seen
by the business world in today's highly competitive recruiting and
placement environment as particularly well fitted to respond to this
widely felt need.

Until the late 1950s, the school was an eminent practitioner of the
3/2-year approach, and it served well. But it did emphasize taking
care of "our men" from Dartmouth (the first female Tuck School student graduated in 1970), losing in the process the diversity and cross-
fertilization of a search for talented undergraduates from all over the

country (and from around the world). But as 3/2 applicants began to compete with a large and talented applicant pool of alumni from Dartmouth and other colleges, as employers began to give clear hiring advantage to the older MBA holders, and as the option of giving up their fourth undergraduate Dartmouth year became less attractive for a number of reasons, desire for the 3/2 program began to diminish in the early 1960s. Sixty-five of 97 in the 1959–60 first-year Tuck School class were Dartmouth undergraduates, but only 11 of the 116 in the first-year class of 1965–66 were undergraduates in their senior year in the college.

There were, incidentally, 171 men in the combined first- and second-year classes in 1959–60; this rose to just 213 in 1965–66. These total numbers point up one of Tuck's most enduring differences from the others in the so-called top ten of today's business schools: Tuck is the smallest, by a significant margin from the next-smallest. Tuck has been preeminent among these schools in the statistics generally considered to measure "loyalty" among its students. For example, the alumni giving percentages of Tuck have consistently stood at the top of all graduate business schools in the country, by a wide margin from the next on the list. These quantitative figures are useful but truly do not measure the qualitative impact that the Tuck environment seems to exert on its members, a feature that has remained predominant throughout the almost one hundred years of Tuck's existence. The Tuck structure encourages the use of team building and small-group approaches, so widely valued today by progressive corporations. The school's recent pioneering in teleconferencing adds to this potential. Curricula among the top ten schools are not significantly different; environments can be.

The 1990s have brought a sharply heightened emphasis on the global business world. In the 3/2 program days, Tuck posted only a modest record here but in recent decades has had a much more sharpened focus on the international environment that goes back to the Edward Tuck perspective at the beginning. It is noteworthy that in the school's very early announcements, in the years right after its founding, there was mention of concepts to be learned regarding "the less developed world." The demands of international business today by their very nature call on the generalists, on those who have a general management focus in their business training. Tuck stands well here.

Tuck School's debts to Edward Tuck—benefactor, supporter, and role model—and William Jewett Tucker—change agent, innovator, and role model, too—are profound. Both demonstrated their interest in and understanding of "the larger meaning of business." Now the Amos Tuck School of Business Administration is coming up to its centennial, one hundred years after the Dartmouth trustees authorized the program on January 19, 1900. With this auspicious occasion, Tuck celebrates its premier role as the first graduate business school in the country and also its dedication to that "larger meaning."

UNIVERSITY PRESS OF NEW ENGLAND publishes books under its own imprint and is the publisher for Brandeis University Press, Dartmouth College, Middlebury College Press, University of New Hampshire, Tufts University, and Wesleyan University Press.

LIBRARY OF CONGRESS CATALOGING-IN-PUBLICATION DATA
Broehl, Wayne G.
    Tuck and Tucker : the origin of the Graduate Business School /
Wayne G. Broehl, Jr.
      p. cm.
   ISBN 0-87451-916-0 (cloth : alk. paper)
   1. Tuck, Edward, 1842–1938.   2. Tucker, William Jewett,
1839–1926.   3. Amos Tuck School of Business Administration—History.
4. Business schools—New Hampshire—History.   I. Title.
HF1134.A74B76   1999
650'.071'17423—dc21   98–52853